CONTINGENT VALUATION OF NONMARKET BENEFITS IN PROJECT ECONOMIC ANALYSIS

A GUIDE TO GOOD PRACTICE

Asa Jose Sajise, Jindra Nuella Samson, Lotis Quiao, Jasmin Sibal, David A. Raitzer, and Dieldre Harder

DECEMBER 2021

ASIAN DEVELOPMENT BANK

6 ADB Avenue, Mandaluyong City, 1550 Metro Manila, Philippines
Tel +63 2 8632 4444; Fax +63 2 8636 2444
www.adb.org

ISBN 978-92-9269-275-9 (print); 978-92-9269-276-6 (electronic); 978-92-9269-277-3 (ebook)
Publication Stock No. TCS210514-2
DOI: http://dx.doi.org/10.22617/TCS2105142

Notes:
In this publication, "$" refers to United States dollars.
The Asian Development Bank recognizes "China" as the People's Republic of China and "Vietnam" as Viet Nam.

On the cover: CVM is a survey-based approach in which respondents state their willingness to pay for nonmarket goods and services. The method has been applied to quantify many types of cost-benefit values of investment projects related to water supply and sanitation, environment, health, tourism, cultural heritage sites, energy and other areas of public policy in both developed and developing countries.

Cover design by Michael Cortes.

Contents

Tables, Figures, and Boxes

Tables

Figures

Boxes

Foreword

Economic analysis plays a key role in ensuring that project investments use resources efficiently and effectively. The Asian Development Bank (ADB) and other international financial institutions are increasingly designing investment projects that provide multiple benefits. Some of these benefits are easily quantified through market-valuation methods that have been refined through decades of practice.

Other benefits and costs, however, emanate from public goods and services for which markets are absent or imperfect, particularly in developing countries. A complementary valuation method is therefore needed to measure these nonmarket values.

One of the most widely used nonmarket valuation approaches is the contingent valuation method (CVM). CVM is a survey-based approach in which respondents state their willingness to pay for nonmarket goods and services. The method has been applied to quantify many types of values, such as improvement in air and water quality, reduction of risk from drinking water or groundwater contamination, access to outdoor recreation and tourism sites, and protection of wetlands.

Although CVM is conceptually simple, much evidence points to a specific set of practices to follow so that it generates reliable results. Codifying these good practices in the context of economic analysis will help users make the best use of this tool when evaluating investment projects.

This resource book is based on the findings of a retrospect study of ADB's CVM practice from 2015 to 2020 and on an extensive literature review of current CVM best practices. It is intended to supplement existing ADB operational guidelines, handbooks, and technical papers on economic analysis of investment projects. It provides a comprehensive guide on the use of CVM—from study planning to sampling, survey design, survey implementation, and data analysis. By enhancing understanding of CVM concepts and principles, this book can help improve the design and conduct of future CVM studies and estimation of willingness to pay. We hope that this study will benefit all CVM practitioners, and improve economic analysis at ADB and beyond.

Joseph E. Zveglich, Jr.
Deputy Chief Economist
Economic Research and Regional Cooperation Department
Asian Development Bank

Acknowledgments

Many individual researchers, economists, and field workers within and outside the Asian Development Bank (ADB) have shared their experiences, learning, and knowledge to support the dynamic and evolving practice of contingent valuation methodology (CVM). This book lays out an extensive review of the good CVM practices available in the literature and distills them to guide ADB's project economic analysis.

This book was undertaken by ADB's Economic Research and Regional Cooperation Department (ERCD) in the hope of contributing to the global knowledge of CVM. It was initiated under the guidance of Rana Hasan, regional economic advisor of ADB's India Resident Mission and former director of the Economic Analysis and Operations Support Division (EREA) of ERCD, and completed under the supervision and support of Lei Lei Song, director of EREA.

The EREA study team led the CVM review process and prepared the manuscript, with Asa Jose Sajise, an independent consultant, as the main author, and with coauthors Jindra Nuella Samson, senior economics officer; Lotis Quiao, national economics officer; Jasmin Sibal, national economics officer; David A. Raitzer, economist; and Dieldre Harder, an independent consultant. Jeffrey Liang, principal economist, provided guidance on the study process. The book also benefited from the extensive peer review of John Weiss, a widely published author in the field of economic analysis; Jaimie Kim Arias, an associate professor at the Department of Economics of the University of the Philippines at Los Baños; Aimee Hampel-Milagrosa, an economist at EREA; and Leonard Leung, an economist at ADB's Southeast Asia Department.

Extensive consultations were conducted within EREA and ADB regional departments during the evaluation process. We are most grateful to ADB colleagues who relentlessly shared project experiences, documents, socioeconomic and willingness-to-pay survey instruments, and helped EREA coordinate the key informant surveys with project consultants and firms. We give special thanks to Lilibeth Manalaysay-Buenavente,

Seung Duck Kim from ADB's Central and West Asia Department (CWRD) and Hao Zhang (formerly from CWRD, now with the PRC Resident Mission); Jie Bai, Jan Hinrichs, Lanlan Lu, Hinako Maruyama, Stefan Rau, Baochang Zheng, and Yun Zhou from the East Asia Department (EARD), and Annabelle Giorgetti (formerly from EARD, now with the Private Sector Operations Department); Maria Carina Tinio from the Pacific Department; Pedro Miguel de Almeida, Pradeep Perera, and Santosh Pokharel, from the South Asia Department; and Alan Baird, Thuy Trang Dang, and Allison Woodruff from the Southeast Asia Department.

We also appreciate the assistance of ADB project consultants and survey firm representatives, who shared useful insights and experiences through interviews and key informant surveys on the use of CVM in ADB. We are grateful to Chris Cheatham, Baomin Dong, Amede Ferre, Michael Fortin, Ruth Francisco, Ray Geer, Myrna Hernandez, Arustan Joldasov, Shikha Shukla, Deepa Tripathi, Jeffrey Weber, and Tim Yates.

This book was funded under Technical Assistance 9693: Strengthening Conduct of Economic Appraisal of Projects and Programs, with support from Maria Rowena Cham and Gee Ann Burac on administrative matters. Tuesday Soriano copyedited the manuscript, and Mike Cortes designed the cover and typeset the layout.

Author Profiles

Asa Jose Sajise

Asa Jose Sajise is a professor at the Department of Economics of the University of the Philippines (UP) at Los Baños, where he has been teaching undergraduate and graduate courses in microeconomic theory and environmental economics since 2003. He is also part of the executive committee and a co-regional director for Luzon of the Economy and Environment Group – Philippines (EEG Philippines). He has worked on a variety of environmental economic issues which include, among others, payment for ecosystem services, impact evaluation of community groundwater irrigation, climate change adaptation in coastal areas, and applications of different economic valuation methodologies on ecotourism, sanitation, agrobiodiversity, and forest conservation. He obtained his bachelor's degree in economics from UP Los Baños and his master's and doctoral degrees in agricultural and natural resource economics from UC Berkeley.

Jindra Nuella Samson

Jindra Nuella Samson is a senior economics officer at ERCD of ADB, where she contributes to various analytical research on agricultural and natural resources, climate change and low-carbon growth, economic analyses of investment projects, and country diagnostic studies. Before ADB, she was an assistant scientist and resource economist at the International Center for Tropical Agriculture, stationed at the International Rice Research Institute in Los Baños, Philippines. She worked earlier as a researcher in various nongovernment organizations conducting environmental impact assessments in the Philippines. She obtained her master's degree in environmental science and bachelor's degree in development economics from the University of the Philippines.

Lotis Quiao

Lotis Quiao is an economics officer at ERCD of ADB. She has been involved in reviewing economic analyses of energy projects, preparing power sector assessments, and other analytical work pertaining to country diagnostic studies. Before joining ADB, she was a consultant at the World Bank. She has a master's degree in development economics from the University of the Philippines.

Jasmin Sibal

Jasmin Sibal is an economics officer at ADB's Economic Analysis and Operations Support Division (EREA), ERCD, where she provides operations support particularly in the review of economic analysis of investment projects and in analytical work related to the preparation of country diagnostic and impact evaluation studies. Before joining ADB, she was a monitoring and evaluation officer for the Philippine Conditional Cash Transfer program at the Department of Social Welfare and Development and a senior research executive at a large consumer market research agency in the Philippines. She was also a research assistant at the University of the Philippines where she coauthored studies on maternal health, adolescent and risk-taking behaviors, and decent work country program in the Philippines. She has a master's degree in demography from the University of the Philippines.

David A. Raitzer

David A. Raitzer is an economist at ERCD of ADB. His work has focused on impact evaluation of development interventions, research on environmental policy challenges and agricultural development constraints, and cost–benefit analysis of agricultural and environmental investments. He has provided input into hundreds of project economic analyses at ADB, and prior to ADB, he applied benefit cost techniques to investments in productivity enhancing technologies and environmental policies at the International Rice Research Institute, Center for International Forestry Research, and the Consultative Group on International Agricultural Research. He holds a master's degree in science from the University of Copenhagen and a bachelor's degree in science from Cornell University.

Dieldre Harder

Dieldre Harder is a freelance consultant who has been doing various research work in the water and sanitation sector for 15 years. She has served as team leader and consultant for several World Bank–Water and Sanitation Program (WB–WSP) projects under the Resources, Environment and Economics Center for Studies, Inc., Coffey International, Center for Advance Philippine Studies, and Academika (Indonesia). She was also a short-term consultant at WB–WSP, at DAI for USAID-funded projects, and at ADB. Her published works focus on the application of the contingent valuation method for biodiversity and sanitation. She holds a master's degree in economics from the University of the Philippines at Los Baños.

Abbreviations

ADB	Asian Development Bank
CAPI	computer-aided personal interview
CE	choice experiment
CM	choice modeling
CV	contingent valuation
CVM	contingent valuation method
DBDC	double-bounded dichotomous choice
FGD	focus group discussion
FTF	face-to-face
KII	key informant interview
MBDC	multiple-bounded dichotomous choice
NOAA	National Oceanic and Atmospheric Administration
OECD	Organisation for Economic Co-operation and Development
PAPI	pen and paper personal interview
PCA	principal component analysis
SBDC	single-bounded dichotomous choice
TEV	total economic value
TTT	time to think
WTA	willingness to accept
WTP	willingness to pay

CHAPTER 1

INTRODUCTION

What Is Nonmarket Valuation and Why Is It Important?

Public sector investment is necessitated by market failure to provide socially optimal levels of goods and services. To understand when this investment is needed, social benefits and costs need to be quantified. In some cases, project benefits are close to markets that facilitate valuation. Benefits arising from the opportunity cost of resources used during implementation of projects, whether these are labor or material inputs, are often tangible and readily monetized.

However, not all goods and services are traded or distributed through markets. Some nonmarket goods and services may have intrinsic worth and do not have an equivalent explicit monetary price, but, they are still widely recognized to have important benefits for which people are willing to pay. Accounting for the value of nonmarket benefits and costs is now recognized as an essential and integral part of the economic analysis of projects. Nonmarket valuation is a set of methods used to measure people's willingness to pay for certain goods and services that are not traded in a market. Improvement in ambient air quality, the conservation of culturally significant tourist sites, and the amenity value of preserved forests are some examples of these goods and services.

Nonmarket valuation is important for many reasons, one of which is that it helps to measure the trade-offs people and governments are willing to make, so as to improve the allocation of private and public resources. Since nonmarket valuation is often applied to environmental goods and services, the value it measures can inform environmental policies to correct market failures. Nonmarket valuation also generates monetary estimates that are easy for policy makers to understand and compare with alternative uses of resources.

Many market failures concern public goods, which are defined as nonrival and nonexcludable in terms of their use or consumption by individuals.[1] Market allocation and pricing for these goods are therefore suboptimal. Nonmarket valuation is one way to assign value to this type of goods and services, so that underinvestment can be corrected. When no proper value estimate is assigned, these public goods and resources may be undervalued, preventing proper comparison with other marketed goods and services.

1 Nonrivalrous means that the goods do not dwindle in supply as more people consume them. Nonexcludability means that the good can be accessed and used by all people.

When market benefits and costs pale in comparison to their nonmarket counterparts, economic analysis that is solely based on market benefits and costs can lead to a wrong assessment of the social viability of the project. Failure to include nonmarketed benefits and costs then lead to misallocation of resources to investments that do not maximize value for society.

Contingent Valuation Methodology in Investment Appraisal

The most widely applied nonmarket valuation technique is the contingent valuation method (CVM). CVM is a stated preference approach that relies on directly asking or eliciting people's value for nonmarketed benefits through a survey. Initially, CVM was used in marketing studies to assess potential demand for new products, but now it is a staple in the toolbox of many environmental economists who conduct valuation of environmental goods and services. Use of the CVM technique has expanded to the field of water supply and sanitation, health economics, tourism, valuation of cultural heritage sites, and other areas of public policy in developed and developing countries.

CVM has been often conducted as part of economic analysis to support binary decisions of whether to approve a project. Valid and robust CVM studies and the willingness-to-pay (WTP) estimates they produce, however, have several uses. The results of a CVM study can be a very powerful project design tool that can determine the appropriate scale, timing, and the nature and type of projects. WTP estimates can also be used in negotiations, i.e., as a discussion tool. For instance, these estimates can be used as the basis for setting tariffs and taxes or as input in the bargaining stages of eco-compensation or payment for ecosystem services schemes.

As early as 1998, the Inter-American Development Bank carried out a review of the use of CVM in its project analysis (Ardilla, Quiroga, and Vaughn 1998). The Asian Development Bank's (ADB) 2017 Guidelines for the Economic Analysis of Projects refer to contingent valuation (CV) as one of the methods that can be used to measure benefits accruing from project investments in the power, water supply and sanitation, urban development, and natural resource sectors. Earlier studies by ADB's Economics Research Department (now Economic Research and Regional Cooperation Department) on CVM application produced a series of technical notes (Choynowski 2002; Gunatilake et al. 2006; Gunatilake et al. 2007) that provided CVM guidelines and good CVM practices.

This material was consolidated and brought together in three chapters of ADB's Practical Guide on Cost–Benefit Analysis for Development (ADB 2013). Although the focus was on the application of CVM in water supply and sanitation projects, the guidelines are also useful in measuring the value of benefits and costs in a wide variety of projects, where markets do not function well.

Despite these resources, the increased use of CVM, however, has not always been accompanied by good practice. Instances of poor practice in CVM have generated controversy and skepticism. To ensure that CVM plays an effective role in supporting decision-making, it is important to continue to distill good practices to ensure that application of the method is reliable.

Organization of This Book

Overall, this resource aims to support CVM practitioners who are engaged to prepare and implement CVM studies as part of investment appraisal. While there have been many recommendations on how to conduct a CVM study, this resource is designed to be more of a resource book of current practices and information on CVM. It is hoped that this book will be helpful to those who are applying the methodology for the first time and those who have substantial experience in its application but want to update their practice.

The different chapters are introduced within the context of the stages in implementing a CVM study. These stages are shown in Figure 1.1. In general, there are five main stages in a CVM study: (i) planning, (ii) designing a sampling strategy, (iii) questionnaire design and pretesting, (iv) conduct of actual CVM survey, and (v) data analysis and reporting. The figure also includes the relevant guide questions for each stage.

Chapter 2 discusses the important activities in planning the CV study. Planning activities—which include building a CVM team, conducting initial scoping or project document reviews, identifying benefits, and choosing the elicitation methodology—are important because they initially set up the overall framework of the CV study, as well as define the study scope and provide essential information for designing the CV survey questionnaire.

The next stage is the design of the sampling strategy, which is discussed in ***Chapter 3***. Topics include identification of the target population and construction of a sampling frame. This chapter also gives an overview of different sampling methods and the calculation of the appropriate sample size.

Chapter 4 shows how to properly design a CV survey questionnaire, taking into account the current best global practices and the context of ADB's project investments. The CV questionnaire is the heart of the CV study. The components of the questionnaire are designed to ensure the truthful revelation of respondents of their valuation of the goods or services produced by a project.

Chapter 5 describes the field implementation of a CV study, from training the field survey staff, pretesting the CV questionnaires, and conducting the actual survey. The quality of data from the CV survey depends largely on a team of well-trained enumerators and field supervisors. Pretesting the initial CV questionnaire is very important; it is an iterative process that allows further refinements of the CV questionnaire. This step is essential to the success of the survey and ensures the quality of data that will be collected from the field. Once the CV questionnaire is finalized it is then administered in the actual field survey.

After the survey data are obtained, they are cleaned and processed prior to analysis. ***Chapter 6*** discusses this process and introduces data analysis techniques. It provides Stata examples of the different regression models used to analyze CV data and computation of the willingness-to-pay (WTP) estimates from CV data.

Finally, ***Chapter 7*** distills good practices into a few simple tools and describes the future importance of CVM.

Figure 1.1: Stages of Implementing CVM in Project Economic Analysis

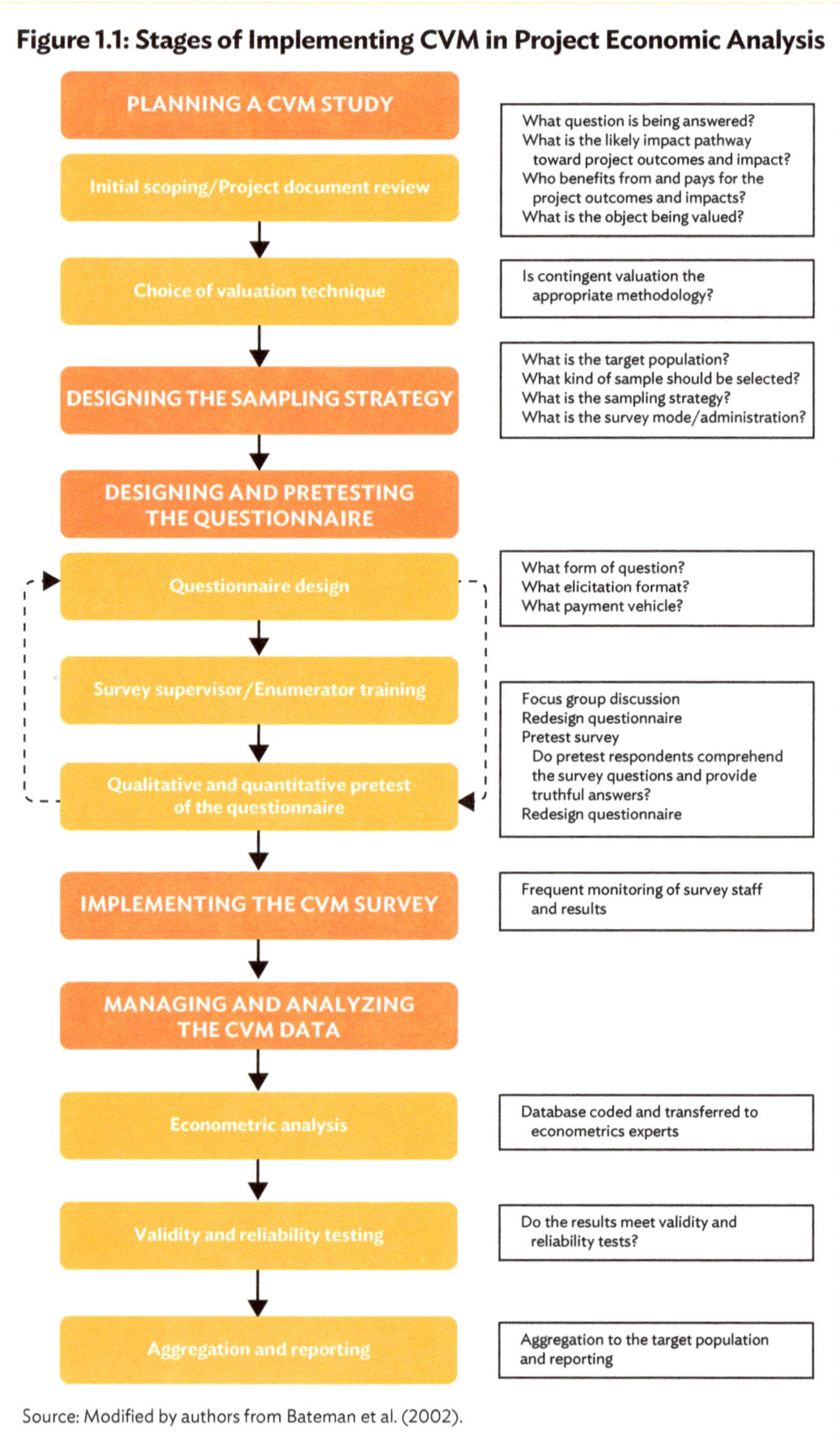
PLANNING A CVM STUDY
Initial scoping/Project document review
What question is being answered?
What is the likely impact pathway toward project outcomes and impact?
Who benefits from and pays for the project outcomes and impacts?
What is the object being valued?
Choice of valuation technique
Is contingent valuation the appropriate methodology?
DESIGNING THE SAMPLING STRATEGY
What is the target population?
What kind of sample should be selected?
What is the sampling strategy?
What is the survey mode/administration?
DESIGNING AND PRETESTING THE QUESTIONNAIRE
Questionnaire design
What form of question?
What elicitation format?
What payment vehicle?
Survey supervisor/Enumerator training
Qualitative and quantitative pretest of the questionnaire
Focus group discussion
Redesign questionnaire
Pretest survey
Do pretest respondents comprehend the survey questions and provide truthful answers?
Redesign questionnaire
IMPLEMENTING THE CVM SURVEY
Frequent monitoring of survey staff and results
MANAGING AND ANALYZING THE CVM DATA
Econometric analysis
Database coded and transferred to econometrics experts
Validity and reliability testing
Do the results meet validity and reliability tests?
Aggregation and reporting
Aggregation to the target population and reporting

Source: Modified by authors from Bateman et al. (2002).

CHAPTER 2
KEY CONSIDERATIONS WHEN PLANNING A CVM STUDY

Key Messages:

- Willingness to pay and willingness to accept are measures that reflect the economic concept of value.
- The concept of the total economic value (TEV) is a useful way to categorize all the benefits (marketed and nonmarketed) that people value.
- Nonmarket valuation techniques can be categorized into direct proxy methods, revealed preference methods, and stated preference methods. Contingent valuation method (CVM) is a stated preference method.
- A valuation method should be selected based on conceptual (i.e., the type/s of benefits being valued in the TEV framework) and practical (budget, time, and skill level) considerations.
- CVM has advantages over other valuation techniques but may suffer from certain biases, of which hypothetical bias is most prominent.
- The choice of elicitation format is critical, as it determines the regression techniques to be utilized to analyze data and determine the sample size and the budget required.
- Different elicitation formats are appropriate to different situations.

Like any method that involves a field survey, a contingent valuation (CV) study requires bringing together inputs and perspectives from different project experts, such as economists, socio-economists, biological and environmental scientists, engineers, and survey field experts. Assembling a competent CV study team and establishing partners with local agencies or authorities (Appendix 1) early in the planning stage is important. Careful thought must be made when deciding to use CVM as a valuation methodology, as the rigor it takes to implement CVM should be weighed against the budgetary and human resources requirements to implement it. CVM requires some level of specialized skills in survey design and econometrics.

The planning stage involves several tasks, which include (i) identification of benefits, (ii) identification of the valuation methodology, and (iii) choice of elicitation format. The information from this stage feeds into the design of the CV questionnaire (see Figure 1.1). The succeeding sections will discuss in detail the tasks to be undertaken when planning a CVM study.

Before a CVM study can be conducted, it is critical to understand the good or service to be valued and who stands to benefit from it. This includes ascertaining the quality and quantity of the good or service with and without an intervention of interest. It also means that the population that will benefit (and/or bear the costs) from the projects, programs, or policies will need to be clearly identified (see Box 2.1 for details of scoping activities).

Box 2.1: Initial Scoping and Project Document Review

The first step in the planning stage is to conduct initial project research and scoping to

a) Understand the rationale behind the investment project, identify the issues or problems the project aims to address, and formulate the specific research questions for the study to answer;
b) Determine the with- and without-project conditions, and identify the specific interventions or output components to be carried out by the project;
c) Establish the impact pathway and possible outcomes of the investment projects, programs, or policies, i.e., how these alternatives can lead to changes or physical impacts that affect human well-being; and
d) Identify affected project areas and the population that will benefit (and/or bear the costs) from the projects, programs, or policies.

To achieve a more meaningful initial project research and scoping, pertinent information must be collected at an early stage through these activities:

a) Review relevant reports/documents for the study design (i.e., sociodemographic profile of target population, maps, related studies, or relevant research performed in the study site, and policies and plans for the proposed program including relevant attributes, common bid or payment range and levels, prior information to inform sample size calculation, etc.).
b) Undertake interviews with key informants and focus group discussions with relevant stakeholders during initial field visits to the project site.
c) Gather available quantitative secondary data from the field such as physical, economic, social, environmental, and health information that may be obtained from national census data as well as municipal or local government records/documents such as a comprehensive land use plan, community-based monitoring system survey, and sector-specific surveys (i.e., forest land occupant surveys), among others.

In ADB projects, the rationale of the project states the challenges and market failures which the project aims to address. Typically, the project components or project alternatives, as well as the project site and beneficiaries will have already been identified before an economic analysis is conducted. For example, some

continued on next page

Box 2.1 (continued)

information about the project is available already at the start of the project's initial consultations, at the project concept paper stage, or when a transaction technical assistance is implemented. The problem tree and impact pathways are often already defined through these preparatory activities. The initial project research and scoping can therefore focus on reviewing these existing project documents with the intent to establish the with- and without-project scenarios, determine the project scope and relevant stakeholder population, and evaluate project impacts, from which costs and benefits can be identified.

Source: Authors.

Identifying Project Benefits

Projects and policies often lead to impacts that affect human well-being. A solid waste management project, for example, can bring about a reduction in water pollution and improve the overall quality of a river. This physical impact can produce multiple benefits like reduced water treatment costs of the water utility, lesser incidence of waterborne diseases, increased recreational activities, or simply a higher level of happiness for people enjoying a pleasant view of the river. All these benefits improve people's welfare, which in turn brings value to the reduction in water pollution. In economics, the concept of value, as discussed in Box 2.2, is linked to the concept of an individual's willingness to pay for the benefit.

When projects produce or use nonmarketed services and goods, it is important to have a framework that will help classify and identify these nonmarket effects and to ensure that these benefits are properly valued and not overlooked or double counted during the project analysis. The framework of the total economic value (TEV) can be a good starting point when capturing a range of possible cost and benefits of a project, and when identifying the proper valuation techniques to be used.

Box 2.2: Review of Basic Economic Concepts Relevant to CVM

It is important to distinguish what is being measured as opposed to how it is measured. Gunatilake et al. (2007), for instance, underscores how basic economic principles on contingent valuation method (CVM) have evolved and demonstrated how these basic concepts have also been muddled in the process. They note that some have called the CVM a willingness-to-pay (WTP) study. To avoid this confusion, they try to distinguish between the concept of WTP, which is the economic value of a good (i.e., the number that is being estimated), and CVM, which is the technique to estimate WTP values.

Value versus Price

The WTP estimate from a CVM study is often misconstrued as the price. Perhaps, the confusion emanates from the fact that the valuation of marketed goods and services in a financial analysis involves multiplying the market price with the quantity of the good or service a project produces. It is important to note that the concept of "value" is different from the concept of "price," as not all goods and services have a monetized price, but all have value. If the price is equated to value, there would be no use for nonmarket valuation since prices already exist. In welfare economics, a good or service will only have value if it enters a person's utility or if it affects his/her utility.

The concept of economic value is also different from the financial accounting of costs and returns of a project or policy. Financial accounting measures out-of-pocket expenses and marketed outputs or benefits. Thus, if a development project's only benefit is time savings from the water collection of women who are not in the labor market, then the project would not have any financial benefit. But if the interest is in the economic benefits of the project, a nonmarket valuation technique may be useful to value these time savings.

The Concepts of Willingness to Pay and Willingness to Accept

A way to measure or deduce how people value goods and services is through the trade-offs they are willing to make. The economic value of a good or service is not what people pay for it but rather how much money they are willing to exchange for that good or service. This exchange can be framed in two ways: (i) willingness to pay (WTP), which is the maximum amount one is willing to pay, if the good or service can be obtained by paying; and (ii) willingness to accept (WTA), which is the compensation one is willing to accept to forgo the good or service.

continued on next page

Box 2.2 (continued)

WTP and WTA are the relevant measures in the economic concept of value. Based on the principles of welfare economics, these concepts take the preferences of individuals as the source of value. To say that an individual's well-being or welfare is better with a development project than without it, is equivalent to saying that the individual prefers a state of the world with the project in it. In terms of exchange, that individual would be willing to pay or exchange some amount of his/her income to be in a state of the world with the project in it. This notion of value is very general in the sense that it can, in principle, be measured for both marketed and nonmarketed goods.

Source: Authors.

The Total Economic Value Framework

In environmental economics literature, the total economic value (TEV) framework has been applied to capture the range of possible project impacts and benefits that people value. The TEV presents the net sum of all the relevant willingness-to-pay and willingness-to-accept values associated with the changes or impacts brought about by a policy or project (Pearce, Atkinson, and Mourato 2006).

The TEV can be decomposed into two main categories, use and nonuse values, as shown in Figure 2.1. Use values refer to the benefits obtained from actual, planned, or probable (future) use of the good or service being valued. These values are further classified into direct, indirect, and future use or option values. Direct use values are benefits that human beings derive from actual use of a good or service. This category also includes nonconsumptive use such as recreation. An example would be the enjoyment of a scenic lake or river, which provides direct satisfaction to human beings but not necessarily through consumption. Indirect-use value, on the other hand, is often associated with natural ecosystem services. These are also called indirect services because they support other biological and ecological processes that indirectly benefit people (Freeman 2003). For instance, a reforestation project that aids in regulating water flow can protect communities from downstream flooding. Another example is a mangrove forest that can provide storm-surge protection, which reduces damage to life and property. Finally, environmental services and goods may have value because they can be a potential source of benefit in the future. Nonuse value, on the other hand, is the satisfaction and value human beings obtain from

Figure 2.1: The Total Economic Value Framework and Valuation Techniques

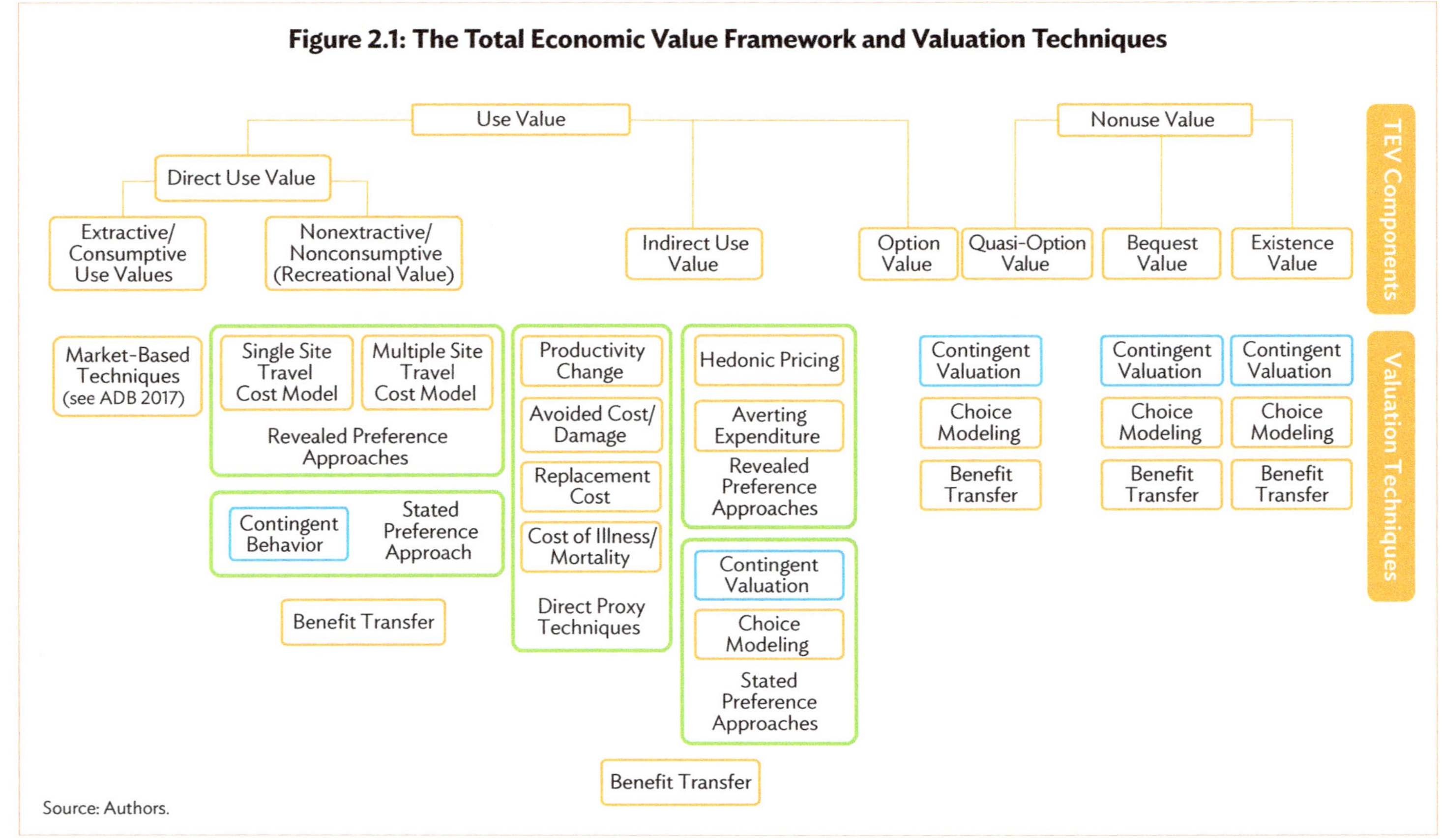
TEV Components
Valuation Techniques
Use Value
Nonuse Value
Direct Use Value
Extractive/ Consumptive Use Values
Nonextractive/ Nonconsumptive (Recreational Value)
Indirect Use Value
Option Value
Quasi-Option Value
Bequest Value
Existence Value
Market-Based Techniques (see ADB 2017)
Single Site Travel Cost Model
Multiple Site Travel Cost Model
Revealed Preference Approaches
Contingent Behavior
Stated Preference Approach
Benefit Transfer
Productivity Change
Avoided Cost/ Damage
Replacement Cost
Cost of Illness/ Mortality
Direct Proxy Techniques
Hedonic Pricing
Averting Expenditure
Revealed Preference Approaches
Contingent Valuation
Choice Modeling
Stated Preference Approaches
Benefit Transfer
Contingent Valuation
Choice Modeling
Benefit Transfer
Contingent Valuation
Choice Modeling
Benefit Transfer
Contingent Valuation
Choice Modeling
Benefit Transfer

Source: Authors.

goods and services apart from their actual, planned, or probable use. For this reason they are also called passive use values. Flores (2003), citing Krutilla (1967), identified three nonuse values: (i) quasi-option value, which is the expected value of new information in cases where actions or decisions may result to irreversible consequences; (ii) existence value, or the value assigned to goods and services simply because they exist; and (iii) bequest value, which is the satisfaction derived by the current generation from bequeathing goods and services to future generations.

Simply put, the TEV is the sum of compatible use and nonuse values an individual assigns to the change resulting from a project or policy. Although it can be desirable to estimate the full TEV of benefits emanating from a development project or a policy, it is often impractical to do so. For one, the tangibility of a value decreases as one moves from use to nonuse values. People may also have less affinity or experience with these more intangible benefits. The absence of affinity or experience often leads to poor expression of value and, hence, uncertain value estimates in CVM studies. Furthermore, there will be outputs like those from water and sanitation projects, for example, where nonuse values will be zero or close to it, so that the full framework will not apply. Box 2.3 tries to illustrate the application of the TEV framework in a nature-based solution project related to treating wastewater discharge and agricultural runoff, as an example.

Box 2.3: Ecosystem Services and Nature-Based Solutions to Wastewater Discharge: Application of the Total Economic Value Framework

River systems are complex ecosystems that provide a myriad of services. They provide provisioning services in the form of harvestable goods, such as fish and other wildlife as well as opportunities for recreation like boating and fishing. These systems also perform regulatory functions, such as the natural dilution of wastewater and natural purification of water. These services can be categorized using the TEV framework (see Figure 2.1). Extraction of fish and other wildlife provide consumptive (direct use) value, while recreation and enjoyment of an aesthetic river view are nonconsumptive (direct use) values. Regulatory functions that ultimately lead to clean or good quality of water can be classified as indirect use values. By producing clean water, these regulatory functions can also be associated with reduced incidence of waterborne diseases. An attractive clean river, finally, may also evoke nonuse value through existence and bequest values. That is, people's utility may be affected by knowing that a clean river exists, not necessarily with the intent of using it (existence value) or because it can be used by future generations (bequest value).

Wetland construction is a type of nature-based solution that can be used to mitigate nonpoint source pollution from agriculture and wastewater discharge. Wetlands act as natural filters, purifying runoff from agricultural wastewater. Their regulatory function, therefore, restores the provision of ecosystem services and the values associated with a clean or restored river ecosystem. The TEV of a restored river system can be credited (partially or wholly) to the regulatory functions (or as an indirect use value) of this nature-based solution.

Nature-based solutions, often also provide many ecosystem services that people may value. Wetlands perform other regulatory services such as water retention for groundwater recharge and flood control. These services are ecological functions that can be classified as indirect use values. They can be a source of food because they provide fish and other wildlife. Recreational activities can also be done in the wetlands. Thus, a set of values associated with wetland construction may include the function of restoring a river ecosystem as shown in the box figure.

continued on next page

Box 2.3 (continued)

Total Economic Value of a Wetland Construction and Restoration of a River Ecosystem

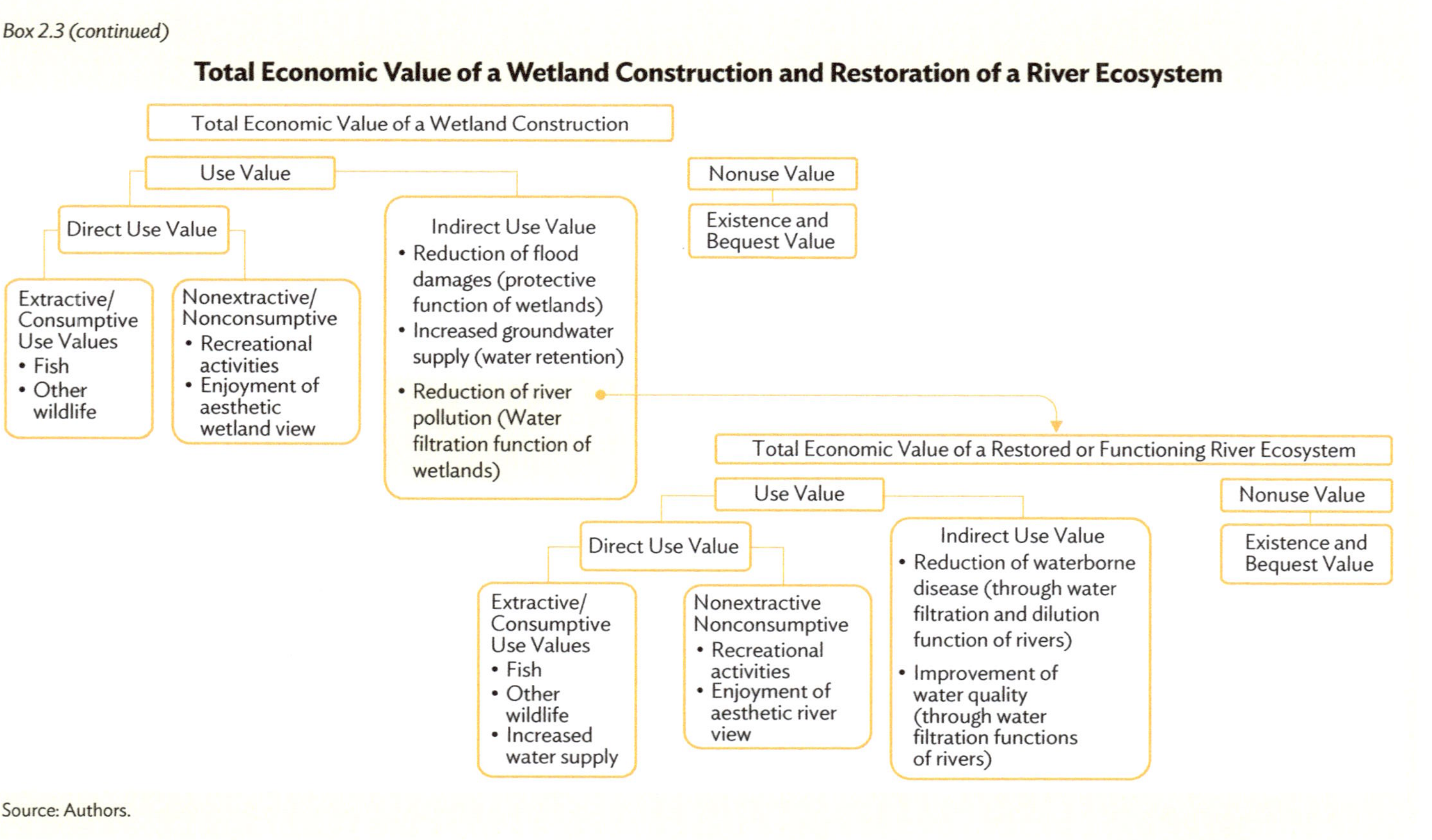

Source: Authors.

Choosing a Valuation Technique

Once the categories of values from project impacts are identified, they need to be matched with appropriate valuation methodologies. There are three general broad categories of nonmarket valuation techniques: (i) direct proxy methods, (ii) revealed preference approaches, and (iii) stated preference approaches. Other terms used for these approaches are indirect methods for revealed preference approach and direct methods for stated preference approach (see, for instance, Perman et al. 2003).[2] Box 2.4 describes the different nonmarket valuation techniques in more detail.

Box 2.4: Nonmarket Valuation Techniques

Direct Proxy Methods (Dose-Response Approach)

Direct proxy methods are used when a marketed good or service can proxy for a nonmarketed one. For example, the benefits from the flood protection services of wetlands can be proxied by the damage costs avoided or the damage that could have been incurred if a wetland was degraded or converted to other land uses. Valuation methods that fall under this category include the productivity change method, replacement costs, damage cost avoided, cost of illness, and cost of premature mortality. These methods all assume that a direct or indirect physical relationship exists between a marketed good (individual's health condition and health expenditures, physical condition of properties and value of property, etc.) and the nonmarketed good or service (flood protection services, water filtration services, etc.). It presupposes some form of an established dose-response function between the marketed good and the nonmarketed good or service.

Productivity Change

Productivity change methods are used when the nonmarketed good or service can be considered an input in the production of a marketed good. The value of the nonmarketed good or service can be inferred from the changes in the production value of the marketed good. For example, the soil erosion control offered by upstream forest conservation can lead to the reduced siltation of irrigation canals, which in turn, can generate increases in crop production downstream. The increase in crop production attributable to this

continued on next page

[2] A caveat is in order, however, as Carson and Louviere (2011) emphasize, the terms revealed and stated preferences are somewhat deceptive in that these methods do not obtain data on actual preferences but rather data from which these preferences can be inferred.

Box 2.4 (continued)

process can be used to value the soil erosion control benefits from the forest conservation project.

Damage Cost Avoided and Substitute Cost

The value of nonmarketed goods and services can also be assessed through the cost of substitute marketed goods or services that provide the same level of benefits. For example, the loss in the protective services of mangroves can be valued through the cost of constructing seawalls or similar infrastructure that can provide an equivalent level of service or benefit at the least cost. Alternatively, the potential cost of damage to life and property in cases where the protective function of a mangrove ecosystem is impaired or lost can be used to value these services.

Cost of Illness or Mortality (Human Capital Approach)

Another way in which a nonmarketed good or service is related to a marketed good is when it is an input in the household production of utility yielding commodities, most prominent of which is health. Two methods for valuing health-related impacts are the cost of illness and cost of mortality (or the human capital approach) approaches, which can be used, for example, in a situation where a project's target is to reduce air pollution and there is sufficient epidemiological evidence that certain health end points are caused by air pollution. The cost of illness approach accounts for both the direct cost (e.g., hospitalization and medical costs) and indirect costs (e.g., value of lost productivity because of work loss days) of being sick because of air pollution. The cost of mortality or human capital approach, on the other hand, calculates the loss of earnings or income streams in the event of a death attributed to air pollution. The avoided cost of morbidity and/or mortality can be used to value the health benefits from the air pollution reduction project.

Revealed Preference Approach

The revealed preference approach relies on observing actual choices and behavior in a related market. For example, the value of the benefits of coral reef conservation can be deduced from people's travel or recreational behavior through the amount they are willing to spend to visit a reef. These methods rely on a "behavioral trail" that can be traced from a well-functioning market to the nonmarketed benefit or goods and services. Commonly used revealed preference methods in valuing nonmarketed benefits include hedonic pricing, travel cost models, and averting or defensive expenditures.

continued on next page

Box 2.4 (continued)

Hedonic Pricing

Hedonic pricing estimates the value of nonmarketed goods and services by linking them to property or labor markets. It uses either spatial or temporal variation in the prices of real estate properties to determine the value of environmental amenities. It recognizes that prices of real estate or houses vary with a bundle of attributes that may include indicators of environmental quality. The value of changes in environmental quality or the benefits from a policy or project that results in these changes is simply that portion of the change in real estate price that can be attributed solely to changes in environmental quality.

Travel Cost Method

The travel cost method is a nonmarket valuation technique that was developed to capture recreational value. It relies on the observation that travel and recreation are weak complements (Pearce, Atkinson, and Mourato 2006) and that travel and access costs are behaviorally equivalent (Perman et al. 2003). The logic is that people will not spend to travel to places that do not increase their utility or welfare.

Defensive Expenditures

This method measures the cost of actions by an individual or household to protect themselves against potential risks or hazards or to mitigate adverse effects of exposure that may cause negative impacts. For example, the value of clean water can be estimated by studying the amount households spend for bottled water. These expenditures "defend" or help them avoid the harmful effects of poor-quality tap water.

Stated Preference Approach

The stated preference approach uses direct questioning, usually through a survey to elicit the willingness to pay for a nonmarketed good or service. This approach asks respondents about their willingness to pay for goods or services, where there is either no market (as for environmental services) or where an existing market is controlled, so the price is not at a market-clearing level (as for various public utilities). Under this category, the two most common methodologies are (i) the contingent valuation methodology (CVM), and (ii) choice modeling or choice experiment.

continued on next page

Box 2.4 (continued)

Contingent Valuation Methodology

CVM was originally used as a methodology to value public goods that bestow some passive use values. Through time, however, its application has expanded beyond environmental economics to health and some utility sectors, among others. In one of the most common forms of CVM, respondents are asked whether they would pay or vote for a proposed change that results in a benefit at a specific cost (or more technically a specific bid). CVM lets respondents state their value or WTP for a change in a hypothetical or constructed market, hence the term contingent valuation—i.e., the value one states is contingent on a constructed hypothetical market.

Choice Modeling or Choice Experiment

Another common type of stated preference approach is choice modeling (CM). Like CVM, respondents are asked directly for their WTP to obtain or WTA to forgo a good or service in a hypothetical change scenario. But unlike CVM, this method seeks to understand how individuals make trade-offs for the different attributes of a good or service. For example, CVM may look at how people value the change from a status quo or baseline level of water quality to an improved water quality level, while CM would look at how people would value a change in the individual attributes of water quality. Hence, respondents make a choice from among the different levels of each water quality attribute. Implicitly, water with different attribute levels is considered a different good. With this method, the analyst can calculate WTP for each individual attribute of the good instead of just the good itself. For instance, instead of obtaining only the WTP for improved water quality in general, the analyst can measure WTP for each water quality attribute such as taste, appearance, and reliability of water service. Appendix 2 provides a more detailed discussion on the design and application of choice modeling as well as the differences and advantages of CVM and CM.

Source: Authors.

The choice of valuation technique is directly related to the type of value or benefit produced by a project. A project or program, however, may be associated with many benefits and thus, require a combination of valuation techniques. Figure 2.1 shows the different techniques that have been commonly applied to measure the different components of the TEV of a project. From the figure, it can be seen that the valuation techniques will first depend on the benefit that is being valued.

Once project costs and benefits are identified, the next step is to select an applicable valuation technique from those shown in Figure 2.1. To make this decision, it is necessary to first consider conceptual issues related to the goal of the valuation study. Practical considerations such as budget, time, and the skills set of the analyst could also influence the choice of valuation technique.

Direct Use Values

Direct use benefits that are consumptive or extractive in nature can be valued mainly through market-based methods. For these benefits, methods to extrapolate consumer surplus from observed price/quantity equilibria to new levels of service provision are clearly described in ADB (2017).

In the valuation literature, the more common nonextractive (or nonconsumptive) direct benefit has been associated with recreational benefits. Recreational value, for instance, is often measured using the travel cost method as the main valuation approach. There are two variants or models of the travel cost method: (i) single site, and (ii) multiple site models. Table 2.1 provides some questions that can help lead to the appropriate choice between the two variants of the travel cost method.

Table 2.1: Questions to Help Decide among the Variants of the Travel Cost Method

Question	Suggested Valuation Techniques
1. Is the interest only in a single recreational site or are multiple sites being considered?	
Single site only (go to question #2)	
Multiple sites	Multiple Site Travel Cost Models (i.e., random utility-based models)
2. Is the site a unique site that visitors often visit only once?	
Yes	Contingent Behavior (a CVM variant)
No	Single Site Travel Cost Models

Source: Authors.

Indirect Use Values

Techniques that measure indirect use values can rely on behavioral responses such as the purchase of a house or purchase of goods and services to protect oneself. These techniques are categorized under revealed preference approaches (see Box 2.4). Finally, indirect benefits can also be valued by using stated preference methods.

For ***indirect benefits*** (or indirect use values) the selection of an appropriate valuation technique is made more complex because there can be many different types of services provided by an intervention. Table 2.2 suggests some questions that may guide the selection of an appropriate technique to value indirect benefits.

Table 2.2: Questions to Guide the Selection of an Appropriate Valuation Technique for Measuring Indirect Benefits

Question	Suggested Valuation Techniques
1. Do the indirect benefits affect the production of marketed goods?	
Yes, production of marketed goods	Productivity Change Method
No (go to question #2)	
2. Do these indirect benefits have attributable health effects (i.e., there is epidemiological proof/basis of associated health effects)?	
Yes	Cost of Morbidity; Cost of Mortality (Human Capital Approach); Contingent Valuation Method
No (go to question #3)	
3. Are these indirect benefits related to replaceable costs or potential damages to property?	
Yes	Avoided Damage Cost; Substitute Cost
No (go to question #4)	
4. Do these indirect benefits affect behavior in the housing market (i.e., purchase of houses) or behavior in "insurance" markets (i.e., purchase of insurance or other protective or "defensive" products)?	
Yes (affects behavior in housing markets)	Hedonic Pricing Method
Yes (affects behavior in insurance or "defensive" markets)	Defensive Expenditure
No	Stated Preference Techniques (see Table 2.1)

Source: Authors.

Nonuse Values

To value nonuse benefits (i.e., option, quasi-option, bequest, and existence values) only stated preference approaches such as CM and CVM are applicable. The stated preference approach is also the most appropriate for valuing goods and services that are unique and evoke cultural values. Therefore, for nonuse values, the choice is typically between choice modeling and the contingent valuation methodology. Table 2.3 presents some questions that can help determine which of these two techniques would be more appropriate to use.

Table 2.3: Questions to Determine which Stated Preference Method to Use

Question	Suggested Valuation Techniques
1. Is the interest in the marginal willingness to pay for individual project attributes?	
Yes	Choice Modeling
No	Contingent Valuation Method
2. Do respondents view the benefits in terms of individual attributes?	
Yes	Choice Modeling
No	Contingent Valuation Method

Source: Authors.

Finally, note that the benefit transfer method appears as a practical option in almost all of the components of the TEV. However, the transfer of values from one study to another requires certain requirements to be met (Appendix 3 gives a more detailed discussion on how to implement benefit transfer methods). Thus, while this method is convenient to use, much caution is needed in using it.

Advantages of the Stated Preference Approach

While the validity of revealed preference approaches is widely accepted, stated preference methods also have many advantages. Although the discussion in this section focuses on CVM, the advantages mentioned here are equally applicable to choice modeling (CM) and other stated preference approaches.

In general, the most notable advantage of stated preference methods is that these are the only methodologies that can measure nonuse or passive use values. Early applications of CVM focused on estimating the conservation and preservation values of natural resources or ecosystems. Stated preference methods can measure use values that are not currently accounted for by existing markets and observed conditions of behavior. At one extreme, there are use values that are associated with externalities, for which there is no market.

For example, sewerage projects often yield considerable positive externalities, such as pollution reduction or environmental amenity improvements. Since markets fail to account for these benefits even though they affect people and improve their welfare, relying only on market-based approaches or on revealed preference approaches may not be adequate.

At the other extreme, there can be markets that are controlled, so there is non-price rationing, and the price people actually pay is well below what they would be willing to pay, such as in the case of subsidized utilities. Thus, one major advantage of stated preference methods is that they can produce estimates of value for goods and services that either are not traded in a market or are traded in a market that is functioning poorly. The methods also have the advantage of, given their correct implementation, being able to accurately estimate value beyond the range of an individual's historic experience (Smith 2007).

Stated preference approaches are also more flexible revealed preference approaches. The impacts of a wide range of projects and policies as discussed earlier may include both use and nonuse benefits or values. Travel cost methods, for instance, can only estimate the values people put on benefits associated with recreational services. In this method, it is necessary to establish the relationship between the environmental good and a marketable good, i.e., a "behavioral trail"; while the revealed preference method requires that the demand for the market good is estimated and the effect of environmental quality on the good must be isolated. Without this behavioral trail, the methods cannot be applied, thus limiting their range of application. Stated preference approaches are direct methods that can be applied without these intermediate relationships. Studies that have compared estimates from revealed and stated preference approaches have concluded that the difference is often statistically insignificant (see Box 2.5 for more discussion).

Another strength of the stated preference approach is that it elicits WTP and WTA directly. Hence, it is related directly to correct measures of welfare or utility changes (Perman et al. 2003). It does not rely on the properties of weak complementarity—which underlie preference approaches—to be a good measure of utility or welfare changes (see, for instance, Bockstael and McConnell 2007). In short, stated preference methods offer a theoretically consistent measure of value or welfare changes without extra assumptions.

Unlike revealed preference approaches, stated preference methods can also be a platform through which various stakeholders affected by a project or policy can communicate and share ideas. As will be discussed later, one good practice is to make the constructed or hypothetical markets as close as possible to the real scenario (Alpizar et al. 2008). To do this, economists must do extensive groundwork, which often involves bringing together and meeting different stakeholders[3] through focus group discussions, to understand the technical and institutional requirements of a policy or project to bring about the desired change or benefit.

Box 2.5: Revealed or Stated Preference? Or Revealed and Stated Preference?

One prominent theme in the valuation literature has been the comparison of revealed and stated preference. Since revealed preference value estimates are obtained from observed behavior it has been used to confirm the validity of stated preference value estimates for CVM. Carson et al. (1996) gave one of the early meta-analyses of stated and revealed preference value estimates for quasi-public goods. They analyzed 83 studies that contained both revealed and CVM estimates for the same good or service. They found that the median CVM-revealed preference ratio ranged between 0.75 and 0.94 with most of the distribution located between 0.25 and 1.25. This implies that CVM estimates were lower relative to the revealed preference estimates. The correlation coefficient between the estimates was also statistically significant and was between 0.72 and 0.92, indicating the convergent validity between the two estimates.

Comparison between the two estimates for a common good or service has continued after the Carson et al. (1996) study (see some of these studies in the box table). Such studies, however, are not very common as they entail a large research budget. For the studies identified in the box table, a statistical comparison was also seldom made; but for studies that made a statistical comparison, the estimates were not found to be statistically different.

Dwelling too much on proving the equivalence of the revealed and stated preference valuation estimates might, however, be counterproductive. For one, the two approaches may measure or are meant to measure different benefits or values in the total economic value framework. Conceptually, since the revealed preference approaches are demand-based estimates, they are more related to consumer surplus (CS) welfare measures. CVM welfare measures, on the other hand, are more related to Hicksian welfare measures of equivalent and compensating surplus, which are not equal to but rather bound consumer surplus values. It has been suggested that a more productive undertaking is to treat the approaches as complementary rather than substitute, which can be a more comprehensive picture of preferences since current behavior captured

continued on next page

3 Stakeholders are individuals, local government units, research agencies, nongovernment organizations (NGOs), or community groups that have relevant information or stake to contribute in project decision-making and implementation.

Box 2.5 (continued)

by the revealed preference approach can be complemented by insights on behavior beyond existing markets from a stated preference approach (Cameron 1992). It can also lead to more efficient parameter estimates and reduced bias (Kling 1997).

Studies that Compared Revealed and Stated Preference Estimates

Authors	Year	Good/ Service	Revealed Preferences Estimate	Stated Preference Estimate	Remarks
Ready, Berger, and Blomquist	1997	Amenity benefits (existence) of Horse Farmland	$0.43 (Hedonic Pricing)	$0.49 (CVM-SBDC)	Difference statistically insignificant
Herath and Kennedy	2004	Recreational value	A$11,128,262 (Aggregate CS - Travel Cost)	A$4,375,000 (Aggregate WTP; CVM - SBDC)	No test for difference
Nam and Son	2005	Recreational value	D45.5 billion (Aggregate CS - Travel Cost	D6 billion (Aggregate WTP; CVM - Payment Card)	No test for difference
Ambrecht	2014	Cultural experience (use values)	€1,558,000 (Aggregate WTP; Travel Cost)	€1,960,000 (Aggregate WTP; CVM - Open ended)	No test for difference
Tidwell	2020	Improvement in Peri-Urban Sanitation	$1.70 (Hedonic Pricing)	$2.60 (CVM - SBDC) $3.40 (Choice Experiment)	Difference statistically insignificant

CS = consumer surplus, CVM = contingent valuation method, SBDC = single-bounded dichotomous choice, WTP = willingness to pay.
Source: Authors.

Stated preference methods are designed to focus on a specific project or program-related change. Hence, as far as environmental effects are concerned, stated preference methods have been developed to measure incremental changes in environmental quality. This means that these methodologies have been developed to study the impacts of development projects or policies on a site or several sites. However, they have not been developed for system-wide changes such as the degradation of the world's oceans or global climate changes (Alberini and Kahn 2006).

Among the stated preference approaches, CM reveals more information than CVM, as it generates WTP for different levels of multiple attributes. Thus, it is more helpful when project design is uncertain and the types and levels of goods and services generated are not yet stabilized. However, for CM to estimate WTP from a given survey, enumeration of the full array of choice sets is needed. Questionnaires that are incomplete are not usable, so the precision of enumeration must be very high. In addition, special software is needed to develop a limited set of choice sets that is orthogonal and from which willingness to pay for levels of attributes can be recovered. In settings where this level of precision is not possible and the main interest is in WTP for a defined good or service, CVM is more appropriate and practical.

Criticisms against Contingent Valuation Methods

Stated preference approaches such as CVM, while having distinct advantages over revealed preference approaches, are not without flaws. After reviewing selected empirical CVM studies, Hausman (2012) concluded that there are three long-standing problems with the methodology: (i) hypothetical bias, (ii) insensitivity to scope, and (iii) disparity or difference between WTP and WTA measures. Other biases have been identified throughout the development of the methodology: information bias, starting point bias, and payment vehicle bias. These latter three biases, however, have been less contentious and are easily addressed through a carefully crafted CV questionnaire (more detailed discussion is in Chapter 4).

Hypothetical Bias

The hypothetical nature of CVM can create what is called a hypothetical bias. List et al. (2004) defined hypothetical bias as simply the difference between hypothetical statements of value and actual valuation by the respondent. The presence of hypothetical bias in CV studies has been extensively studied, for example, in studies where respondents assigned to a hypothetical treatment group are told that the valuation exercise is purely hypothetical, while another group is presented with a scenario that involves actual payments. Several studies validate the presence of hypothetical bias, where mean hypothetical WTP is higher than mean WTP from actual payments.

In field settings, the bias emanates from the context that respondents base their WTP statement on a hypothetical scenario. This may lead to either an overstatement or understatement of their stated value relative to the true value for the good or service from a project or policy. Respondents may state that they will be paying for the good in the hypothetical scenario but will not do so in reality or will pay a lower amount in a similar real-life purchase decision. Understatement can occur in questions related to the costs of paying to mitigate damages, such as cleaning oil spills or other environmental damage.

There could be several reasons for non-truthful revelation of value under a CV's hypothetical scenario. One possible reason is that respondents do not find the posited scenario to be "consequential" to them. A survey elicitation is consequential if respondents view that they may need to actually pay the stated amount when answering the elicitation question in order for the good or service to be provided. Carson and Groves (2007) argue that CV surveys need to be framed consequentially so that respondents will pay attention to the alternatives and believe that the institution/agency who will provide the good will consider their response when making decisions. For instance, asking tourists if they are willing to pay for a surcharge in entrance fees in return for experiencing future improvements in a recreational site may be an inconsequential scenario. This is because these tourists may feel that such improvements and the surcharge may not affect them if they have no plans of returning to the recreational site in the future. Another reason is excessive yea-saying. Yea-saying is the tendency of the respondent to agree or, in the case of CVM, affirm their willingness to pay even if in reality they are not willing to do so.

Hypothetical bias is also associated with strategic bias. Strategic bias is a product of the respondent resorting to strategic behavior to influence the results of the study to receive a desired outcome. Arrow et al. (1993) forwarded the concern that incentive structures associated with various payment mechanisms may influence willingness-to-pay values. A common example is a hypothetical scenario asking for voluntary contributions to a program that will improve environmental quality, say air quality, which is a public good. Studies show that there is an incentive to free ride and overstate WTP under such a hypothetical scenario (Carson et al. 1997; Carson and Groves 2007). This is especially acute when respondents feel that they will not pay but have the chance to influence the actual provision of the public good through an overstated WTP. Conversely, the understatement of WTP is also possible if, for example, respondents are faced with voluntary contributions for a highly desirable public good. In this instance, there is an incentive to understate true WTP given that they can free ride.

Hypothetical bias, however, may be more pronounced for public goods and goods with which respondents are less familiar. For water improvements, for instance, hypothetical bias would be less of a problem (Gunatilake 2007) compared with improvements in biodiversity levels. People may have a limited notion of what biodiversity is to start with and therefore would have no concept of how changes in its levels would affect their utility.

Scope Insensitivity[4]

CVM-derived values need to be sensitive to the scope of the project or policy benefits. Insensitivity to scope occurs when respondents are willing to pay the same amount for goods that differ in quantity, yet willing to pay different amounts for the same goods valued under different conditions, which are believed to be "neutral" or should have no influence over the amount people are willing to pay (Carson and Mitchell 1995).

It can also happen when a policy or a project has an extensive geographic scope. Respondents may value the independent policy or project impacts differently from the joint impacts. In the case of geographically extensive project impacts, respondents may value the impacts differently when regions are subdivided than when impacts are taken for the whole region. Studies have reported mixed results on the scope insensitivity problem. Kahneman, Knetsch, and Thaler (1990); Boyle et al. (1998); and Svedsäter (2000) confirm that CV estimates are sensitive to scope, while others show insensitivity to the scope of the good being valued.

WTP and WTA Disparity

In theory, the WTA and WTP measures of welfare or value should be similar. However, lab experiments as well as field estimates have shown a large disparity between these two measures with WTA estimates being higher. Earlier CVM guidelines (Arrow et al. 1993) recommended the use of WTP over WTA because WTP was bounded by income and would tend to be more conservative. But there are situations where WTA would be more appropriate especially when valuing damages or determining compensation from injury. Several explanations have been put forward to explain the significant disparity between the two measures of value.

[4] Insensitivity to the scope is also referred to as the "embedding" effect or bias (Veisten 2007) and also as the "part-whole bias" (Kahneman 1986).

Apart from the three criticisms mentioned above, the following other biases were also observed in the course of applying the methodology. These other biases are less worrisome both from a field and theoretical perspective.

Information Bias or Framing Bias

Information or framing bias stems from the observation that the type and quality of the information provided to respondents about a public or private good can strongly influence their willingness to pay especially under conditions of high personal relevance (Bergstrom, Stoll, and Randall 1989; Blomquist and Whitehead 1998; Hoehn and Randall 2002). Azjen, Brown, and Rosenthal (1996) noted that WTP for a public good of low importance is higher when framed in an altruistic rather than in an individualistic perspective. Subtle contextual clues can also bias WTP estimates.

Starting-Point Bias

This is the observed tendency for respondents to rely or base their willingness to pay or value for the good or service on the initial bid that is offered. It is also sometimes referred to as the anchoring effect. This bias occurs when the suggested bid level in the dichotomous choice and bidding game elicitation format influences estimates. Respondents would often interpret the starting point in a bidding game as conveying information about the value of the good.

Payment Vehicle Bias

The payment vehicle is a crucial element in the application of contingent valuation because it provides the context for payment. Hence, the choice of payment vehicle (e.g., tax, utility bills, voluntary contributions) could affect the stated WTP. This is especially true if respondents are unfamiliar with the use of tax levies and referenda, which affects the credibility of payment vehicles, thus leading to payment vehicle bias (Morrison et al. 2000). Another reason is when there is a general dislike of the payment vehicle chosen (i.e., increase in utility bills).

Strategies to Reduce Bias

The evolution and development of CVM has largely been driven by the need to address the criticisms against it. These criticisms, as discussed in the previous sections, have been seen to bias estimates from CVM applications. Prominent among these criticisms is the concern that estimates may be unreliable because of hypothetical bias. Initial guidelines came from the National Oceanic and Atmospheric Administration (NOAA) (1993), which were subsequently updated more recently by the reviews of Johnston et al. (2017) and the Organisation for Economic Co-operation and Development (OECD) (2018). These recommendations are taken from publications in peer-reviewed journals. In a nutshell, the general aim of the CVM study is to "present respondents with an incentive-compatible valuation exercise that involves a plausibly consequential decision" to minimize hypothetical and strategic bias as well as respondents' aberrant response behaviors (Johnston et al. 2017, p. 344).

Addressing the biases can be done mainly through a carefully crafted CV questionnaire and good survey strategies for administering this questionnaire in the field. Table 2.4 summarizes the various CVM-associated biases and the current mitigating strategies meant to address them. The succeeding sections of this chapter delve more in detail on each of these bias mitigation measures. A caveat is in order though. Contingent valuation is still a very dynamic and evolving methodology. Current guidelines reflect the best information to date, and these are by no means etched in stone. Actual applications are more nuanced and field- and context-dependent.

Some important CVM terminology used in Table 2.4 of this chapter, and also those that recur throughout this book is defined in the glossary section found at the back of this book.

Table 2.4: Current Best Practices to Mitigate CVM-Associated Biases

Bias and Critiques against CVM	Current Best Practices to Mitigate Bias in CVM
Hypothetical bias: difference between hypothetical and actual statements of value	• Conduct focus group discussion (FGD) and pretesting of questionnaire to understand the context and the good, and preference of respondents • Use of cheap talk scripts or oath scripts • Contingent valuation (CV) scenario must have a well-defined description of a reference level (status quo or baseline) compared with a target level (state of the world with the proposed policy change) of each attribute • Use of referendum approach • Use of debriefing questions to identify protest votes and correction for uncertainty • Assess validity of willingness-to-pay (WTP) estimates
Strategic bias: respondents strategizing to influence results with the intention to free ride when the project is implemented	• Well-designed survey questionnaire • Recommended use of single-bounded dichotomous choice (SBDC) elicitation format • Use of provision point mechanism in CV scenario
Scope insensitivity/embedding effect: expressing the same WTP for goods that differ in quantity yet different WTP for the same goods valued under different conditions Sensitivity of WTP to the order or sequence of the good being valued	• Avoid misspecification of the goods being valued • Use a credible market scenario • Choose nested goods with differences that respondents can easily understand and distinguish • Conduct surveys that engage respondents to carefully think of their response, with a large sample to allow rejection of reasonable differences • Use simple but more powerful statistical tests to detect scope sensitivity
Information bias/framing bias: strong influence of information provided about the good on WTP especially under conditions of high personal relevance	• Provide accurate, plausible, and well-organized information in the CVM questionnaire • Conduct pretesting of questionnaire • Train enumerators
Starting-point bias: anchoring of stated WTP on bid level provided in a dichotomous choice and bidding game elicitation format	• Ensure appropriate elicitation format, decide on the bid levels carefully through desk research, FGDs, and pretesting • Recommended use of SBDC elicitation format whenever applicable
Payment vehicle bias: lack of familiarity or dislike of the payment vehicle affecting stated WTP	• Conduct pretesting of questionnaire • Use debriefing questions to identify and correct protest votes
Interviewer bias: interviewers affecting the choice of respondents	• Train enumerators on neutrality
Sampling bias: sample not representative of target population; Sample may exclude subgroups that are not relevant to the study.	• Random sampling • Stratum should include subpopulation of interest

Source: Authors.

Choosing an Elicitation Format

What Are the Options Available to Elicit Willingness to Pay?

A contingent valuation exercise critically rests on how a single question—the question that elicits the respondent's willingness to pay for the good, service, or amenity of focus—is prefaced and posed. Although the elicitation question needs to be refined during development of the data collection exercise and survey forms, the format of the question needs to be considered early, as it conditions the analytical techniques that can be used, as well as the sample size and resources required. The basic options for eliciting willingness to pay for a described amenity, good, or service are as follows.

- **Dichotomous choice:** The respondent is asked if she or he is willing to pay a randomly determined amount. If only one amount is asked, this is "single bounded." If a follow-up amount based on the first choice is asked (a higher amount if the first answer is "yes" and otherwise a lower amount), this is "double bounded."

- **Payment card:** The respondent is presented with a predetermined set of options and is asked to select one that reflects her or his willingness to pay.

- **Multiple-bounded dichotomous choice:** Multiple bid values are presented as in a payment card, but the respondent indicates levels of certainty of bid acceptance for each level.

- **Bidding game:** The respondent is asked about her or his willingness to pay a small amount, which is increased in successive questions until the respondent is no longer willing to pay.

- **Open ended:** The respondent is allowed to state whatever value she or he wants as willingness to pay.

As summarized in Table 2.5, each elicitation format has advantages and disadvantages (Carson et al. 2001; Pearce et al. 1994; Nunes and Nijkamp 2006; OECD 2018). A watershed conservation project in Mt. Mantalinghan Protected Landscape in the Philippines is used as a hypothetical example to illustrate the differences in the elicitation formats.

Implications for Data Analysis

It should be noted that the format chosen will determine the regression technique used to retrieve respondent willingness to pay. More details of the preferred regression techniques are discussed in Chapter 6, while all other techniques are in Appendix 7.

- The answer to the single-bounded dichotomous choice (SBDC) question is yes/no for a single value. WTP is recovered from SBDC formats using a logit regression, with amount as an independent variable, and acceptance as the dependent variable. The double-bounded dichotomous choice (DBDC) is similar, but uses a bivariate probit.
- In the case of a payment card, the response is an ordered category or interval. WTP is recovered from these formats using an ordered logit, Tobit, or interval regression of WTP category against respondent characteristics. The multiple-bounded dichotomous choice (MBDC) format uses similar methods.
- Bidding games or open-ended questions give a continuous value as a response, and may use ordinary least squares regression, or Tobit techniques if censoring is involved.

Considerations When Choosing a Format

All else being equal, the SBDC format has been found to perform best in many contexts, as it has fewer problems of anchoring or incentive compatibility. At the same time, there are important trade-offs.

SBDC techniques tend to require the largest sample sizes, as only one bid is elicited from each respondent, and the regression technique needed to reveal WTP is somewhat inefficient. They also require that bid amounts can be effectively randomized in the questionnaires administered, which requires a unique questionnaire per respondent. This is most easily achieved when data collection is computer assisted. A carefully considered bid range and distribution is also necessary to avoid anchoring effects. It should be noted that the referendum voting format used for SBDC is also most applicable in democratic governance settings where respondents are accustomed to such voting. DBDC formats on the other hand require smaller sample sizes than SBDC formats, as twice as many bids are elicited per respondent.

Payment card formats are simpler to implement than SBDC or DBDC, require smaller sample sizes, and are amenable to adjustment for population characteristics. But they are also more prone to anchoring, range bias, and strategic behavior. MBDC formats have properties that are not yet well understood, but may help to address some of these issues.

In general, open-ended questions are very far from actual consumer payment situations and are highly susceptible to protest responses and other nonresponses as well as outliers. Bidding games are prone to anchoring bias, may magnify strategic bias, and are subject to respondent fatigue from repeated questioning. For these reasons, both formats have been found to perform poorly than SBDC or payment card methods, and have not been recommended especially when valuing public goods.

Table 2.5: Types and Examples of Elicitation Formats

Elicitation Format	Example	Advantages	Issues
Open-ended	What is the maximum amount you would be prepared to pay every year, through an increase in water surcharge, to protect, rehabilitate, and manage the watershed in the Mt. Mantalinghan Protected Landscape in the ways I have just described?	• Straightforward • Simple to deal with in terms of statistical techniques (simple descriptive statistics can be enough, such as sample means and medians) • Not prone to anchoring or starting point bias[a] • Very informative as maximum WTP can be identified for each respondent	• Lack of familiarity with consumers since it does not reflect actual market transactions, i.e., people deciding if they will buy the good or not at given prices, rather than stating maximum WTP values. • Prone to strategic behavior • Leads to large nonresponse rates, protest answers, zero answers, and outliers (i.e., unrealistically high amounts), and generally too unreliable responses[b] (Mitchell and Carson 1989). • Difficult to use effectively in valuing public goods because respondents want to know what others in the community are going to pay before they give an answer. They may not want to pay more than what is fair even if they strongly prefer the public good more than other people.
Bidding game[c]	Would you pay ₱5 every year, through an increase in water surcharge, to protect, rehabilitate, and manage the Mt. Mantalinghan Protected Landscape in the ways I have just described? If Yes: The interviewer keeps increasing the bid until the respondent answers No. Then maximum WTP is elicited. If No: Interviewer keeps decreasing the bid until the respondent answers Yes. Then minimum WTP is elicited.	• Respondents get some assistance to arrive at a WTP value • Simplified choice process reduces the number of nonresponses • Helps facilitate respondents' thought processes, hence, encouraging them to consider their preferences carefully	• Prone to starting point bias[d] and anchoring bias[e] on initial bid amounts • Leads to many outliers (i.e., unrealistically high bids • Prone to "yea-saying"[f] • Repeated questioning may annoy, tire, or bore respondents, causing them to say "yes" or "no" to a stated amount in hopes of terminating the interview, resulting in less accurate WTP results.

continued on next page

Table 2.5 (continued)

Elicitation Format	Example	Advantages	Issues
Payment card	Which of the amounts listed below best describes your maximum willingness-to-pay every month, through an increase in the water surcharge to protect, rehabilitate, and manage the Mt. Mantalinghan Protected Landscape in the ways I have just described? ₱0 ₱9 ₱20 ₱45 ₱5 ₱10 ₱25 ₱50 ₱6 ₱12 ₱30 ₱60 ₱7 ₱15 ₱35 ₱70 ₱8 ₱18 ₱40 ₱80…	• May avoid starting point bias • Reduces outliers • More informative of the respondents' WTP • Cheaper to implement	• Prone to biases relating to the range of numbers used in the card and the location of the benchmarks, i.e., range bias, centering bias, and end-point bias • Vulnerable to strategic behavior • Respondents might limit their announced WTP to the values listed on the card.
Single-bounded dichotomous choice	Would you vote for the proposal to protect, rehabilitate, and manage the Mt. Mantalinghan Protected Landscape in the ways I have just described if its passage would cost you ₱10 every month, through an increase in your water bill? (The amount is varied randomly across the sample.)	• Simplifies cognitive tasks faced by respondents due to their familiarity. It mimics actual market transactions people make (i.e., take it or leave it or deciding to buy a good at a certain price) • Minimizes nonresponse and avoids outliers	• Prone to anchoring effect or starting-point bias • Provides less information from each respondent[h] • Responses are more difficult to interpret, hence, requiring a larger sample and sophisticated econometric techniques and assumptions to obtain sufficiently accurate information. • May not be applicable in other cultural settings where bargaining is not a norm[i] • Prone to some degree of yea-saying • Expensive to implement in terms of time and resources • Results are highly sensitive to statistical assumptions made.

continued on next page

Table 2.5 (continued)

Elicitation Format	Example	Advantages	Issues
Single-bounded dichotomous choice	For instance, five chosen bid amounts will be distributed randomly across the sample: ₱10, ₱30, ₱50, ₱100, ₱50	• Provides incentive for the truthful revelation of preferences under certain circumstances (i.e., it is in the respondent's strategic interest to accept the bid if his/her WTP is greater or equal than the price asked and to reject it otherwise) • Can be framed as a referendum on a vote for the provision of public goods where respondents may be hesitant to pay more than what they think is fair[g]	
Double-bounded dichotomous choice	Would you vote for the proposal to protect, rehabilitate, and manage the Mt. Mantalinghan Protected Landscape in the ways I have just described if its passage would cost you ₱10 every month, through an increase in your water bill? (The amount is varied randomly across the sample.) If Yes: And would you pay ₱15? If No: And would you pay ₱5?	• Same as a dichotomous choice but more statistically efficient since it provides extra information obtained from the second, open-ended question	• All limitations of the single-bounded dichotomous choice apply. • The danger that the respondents' exposure to the first offer would influence them to accept the follow-up offer. • The complexity of the estimation procedures (see Appendix 7) • Possible loss of incentive compatibility since respondents may not view the second question as separate from the initial Yes/No question

continued on next page

<table>
<tr><th>Elicitation Format</th><th>Example</th><th>Advantages</th><th>Issues</th></tr>
<tr>
<td>Multiple-bound dichotomous choice</td>
<td>This is similar to a payment card except that respondents are asked about their degree of certainty of paying for each bid level:

How probable is it for you to vote for the proposal to protect, rehabilitate, and manage the Mt. Mantalinghan Protected Landscape in the ways I have just described if its passage would cost you the following surcharges to your water bill?

<table>
<tr><th>Bid</th><th>Definitely No</th><th>Probably No</th><th>Not Sure</th><th>Probably Yes</th><th>Definitely Yes</th></tr>
<tr><td>0</td><td>A</td><td>B</td><td>C</td><td>D</td><td>E</td></tr>
<tr><td>10</td><td>A</td><td>B</td><td>C</td><td>D</td><td>E</td></tr>
<tr><td>30</td><td>A</td><td>B</td><td>C</td><td>D</td><td>E</td></tr>
<tr><td>50</td><td>A</td><td>B</td><td>C</td><td>D</td><td>E</td></tr>
<tr><td>100</td><td>A</td><td>B</td><td>C</td><td>D</td><td>E</td></tr>
</table>
</td>
<td>• Directly incorporates uncertainty in the respondent’s valuation decision process
• Reduces the burden of optimal bid design
• Respondents behave more rationally when the choice set (payment bids) is visible throughout the choice tasks
• Improves statistical efficiency of parameter estimates
• Requires lower sample sizes</td>
<td>• Because the approach is relatively new little is known about its incentive compatibility properties and the bid design effects it creates, i.e., anchoring, etc.</td>
</tr>
</table>

continued on next page

Table 2.5 (continued)

WTP = willingness to pay.

[a] Does not provide respondents with cues about what the value of the change might be.

[b] Respondents have difficulty stating their true maximum WTP especially if the change is unfamiliar and one they have never thought of valuing before.

[c] Since the bidding game initially starts with a dichotomous choice question, the choice of the initial bid may come from literature reviews of similar studies, which are verified through groundwork and pretesting. This is the same as the maximum bid.

[d] The final WTP amount at the end of the bidding game is systematically related to the initial bid value.

[e] Respondents who answer the second question may be influenced by the amount specified in the first question (especially if they said yes to the lower amount, their response may be "anchored" to the first amount.

[f] This means that respondents accept to pay the specified amounts to avoid the socially embarrassing position of having to say no. They tend to agree with increasing bids regardless of their true valuations (Kanninen 1995).

[g] The scenario description may specify that all members of the community will be required to purchase the public good at the specified price.

[h] The researcher only knows whether WTP is above or below a certain amount. An opt-out option such as don't know or no answer are included.

[i] A single yes/no question may be considered somewhat rude; hence, respondents may reveal little about their "true" willingness to pay.

Source: Authors.

CHAPTER 3
DESIGNING THE SAMPLING STRATEGY

Key Messages:

- Identifying the relevant survey population depends on the research problem which the CV study intends to address.
- Selecting a sample size that considers adequate power and effect sizes for hypothesis testing is important.
- Probability sampling either through stratified or cluster sampling is recommended.
- CV surveys can be administered in different modes, each having advantages and disadvantages in terms of the cost, potential coverage, and response rates.

CVM, by definition, requires the collection of new data through a survey, and the survey requires a sample to be drawn. The sampling strategy addresses the questions of who and how many to interview. Formulating a good sampling strategy is essential because the representativeness of the sample has implications for the latter implementation stages of CVM. Specifically, the validity of the aggregation of the results to the population rests on the representativeness of the sample.

The sampling strategy should also be articulated when reporting the results of the CV study. The sampling strategy report should include, at the minimum, the population that was sampled, the sampling frame that was used, the sampling method, and the number of sample nonresponse (e.g., refusals) (Arrow et al. 1993). These elements should also be included in the sampling strategy design.

Identifying the Relevant Population and Preparing the Sampling Framework

The first component of a sampling strategy is the identification of the study's population from which a sample will be drawn. The population will vary depending on the research problem or issue which the CV study wishes to address. A CV study on sewerage, for example, may consider its population as those who will be served by the proposed project. Here, geographic considerations may be a primary criterion for identifying the population. Although there are no hard and fast rules for this component, it is best to consider as population of interest all stakeholders who will be affected or impacted by the project or policy. Perhaps a simple question to guide the selection of population is, "Who will pay for and benefit from the project or policy?" (Champ 2003).

The next step is to construct a sampling frame from which a sample will be drawn. A sampling frame is simply a list from which respondents or sampling units are chosen. An ideal sampling frame is one that resembles the closest approximation of the identified target population and allows sufficient representation of subgroups of special interest to the study (Pearce and Ozdemigrolu 2002).

Identifying the population and drawing of the sampling frame are undoubtedly interrelated and primarily driven by the research question underlying the CV study. Thus, these should be part of the groundwork for any CV study. The nuances of identifying the population and the sampling frame are best shown in an example (Box 3.1).

Box 3.1: Sampling Design – Population and Sampling Frames

In 2001, Lauria et al. (2001) conducted a study to obtain accurate and reliable information on household demand for improved sanitation and why households would or would not want improved sanitation services in Calamba, Philippines. Based on the research question or objectives, the study identified the population of interest as households that may be affected by improved sanitation in the area. The research focus was further narrowed down through extensive groundwork consisting of several focus group discussions, key informant interviews, and use of secondary data. Through this groundwork, the research team found that most households already had piped water connections and owned flush and pour-flush toilets. Households were also already satisfied with their on-site sanitation situation. Focus group discussions and pretests also revealed little demand for public latrines. Thus, the apparent remaining sanitation issue or concern was related to the removal of wastewater and the treatment of the waste before disposal into surface water bodies. The development of the CV scenario for the study was simplified as a result.

Practical considerations also helped narrow down further the population of interest to households that owned houses and had pour-flush or flush toilets because they would be in a position to decide on whether to connect to a sewer line. It was also necessary to bound the target population because there were sparsely populated areas on which implementing the focused intervention was not practical. The researchers used two-stage stratified sampling, with each stages requiring a different sampling frame. The first stratification used

continued on next page

Box 3.1 (continued)

a sampling frame of barangays[a] characterized by their population densities and predominant land use. The first-stage sampling frame was constructed from land-use maps and secondary data on barangay population and density. The second stage involved a random selection of households from the selected barangays. The sampling frame for the second stage came from the list of households from the National Statistics Office in Calamba and the local barangay captains.

[a] Barangay is the smallest administrative or political unit in the Philippines. It is similar to a village, district, or ward in other countries.
Source: Lauria et al. (2001).

Sampling Methods

Another integral component of the sampling strategy for a CV study is the process or specific rules of drawing the sample from the sampling frame or the sampling method.

Probability Sampling

The preferred rule in almost all CV studies is to use probability sampling, which gives the members of the sampling frame an equal chance of being chosen. The most basic approach is to use a simple random sampling, which takes at random a specified number of samples from the list. If, for instance, N households will be chosen in the list, then each household would have an equal probability of being chosen, which is equal to 1/N. This can be done by randomly selecting every nth household in the list, drawing the names of the respondents from a covered box, or using random number generators.

Stratified Sampling

Stratified random sampling begins by dividing the entire sampling frame into mutually exclusive strata. The strata can be geographically based, for instance, between rural and urban areas. It can also be based on specific characteristics of the population, for example, foreign and local tourists or income categories in the population. The advantages of stratified random sampling over simple random sampling are that in the context of a CV study, (i) it permits estimation of WTP based on a particular subpopulation; (ii) it may lead to lower survey costs; and (iii) it can increase the efficiency of estimates (Ben-Akiva and Lerman 1985). It should be noted, however, that estimates of WTP for different subpopulations will need to be considered as part of sample power calculations, as they increase sample sizes needed.

Cluster Sampling

Cluster sampling involves dividing the sampling frame into clusters. However, unlike stratified sampling, only a subset of clusters will be selected. That is, the clusters themselves are sampled first. From these selected clusters, household units are then proportionately sampled. For example, villages can first be selected randomly, then from these selected villages household units are chosen randomly. The advantage of this sampling approach is that it also lowers survey costs relative to a simple random sampling; it is also cheaper and easier to sample five households in a village than five households in different villages. It is also practical when no overall sampling frame is available (Pearce and Ozdemigrolu 2002). The sampling frame can be generated only for the clusters that are chosen, thus, saving resources and time by focusing on constructing smaller sampling frames. However, the drawback of cluster sampling is the increased tendency to have higher variances of estimators because respondents in the same cluster most likely have similar characteristics (Bena-Akiva and Lerman 1985).

Systematic Sampling

Systematic sampling is another sampling method that can be employed in the field. Respondents or households are drawn in a deterministic way. For example, a rule of interviewing every fifth house in a block is an example of systematic sampling. If starting points are random there would be no difference between this sampling approach and a simple random sampling, wherein respondents are drawn from a constructed sampling frame.

The choice of sampling design is often based on theoretical criteria. The conventional criterion is to select the sampling approach that minimizes the variance of the parameter estimates. However, this may not be straightforward for CV studies. CV studies are part of the class of discrete choice models, and the problem with these models is that unlike standard linear regression, the variance of parameter estimates for these models depends on the true parameters themselves. Thus, no theoretical result can guide the selection of sampling design, and practical problems such as nonresponse, data reliability, and survey costs may outweigh theoretical issues (Ben-Akiva and Lerman 1985).

Determining the Sample Size

The sample size is also an important component of the sampling design.[6] It is important because the precision of estimates affects their usefulness for policy, and statistical precision affects validity and reliability tests of alternate contingent valuation designs (Boyle 2003). Sample size calculation for discrete choice problems[7] is designed to minimize the error in the choice proportions of the alternatives offered in a study (Rose and Bliemer 2013).

As noted earlier, the sample size needed is conditioned by the elicitation format. SBDC formats need larger samples than DBDC formats, and payment card methods need comparatively smaller samples. Sample sizes are smaller if the sampling is representative. When samples are not fully representative of the beneficiary population, the estimated coefficients need to be used to adjust WTP estimates. To ensure that the estimated coefficients are significant and precise enough for this purpose, larger samples are needed. In addition, subgroup analysis increases the sample size, as estimates should be significant for each subgroup of interest.

For SBDC formats, Hensher, Rose, and Greene (2005) use the following formula[8] to calculate the minimum sample size for a simple random sample. The minimum sample size (N_m) is the one that achieves an allowable or desired deviation between the estimated proportion ($\hat{p}$) and the true proportion (p), with probability greater than or equal to a set confidence level (β). This deviation is expressed as a percentage (a) of the true proportion, i.e., *ap*. The true proportion (p) considered here is equivalent to the proportion of the population that will support the proposed program that would lead, as described by the CV scenario, to changes in the goods or services. The derived formula is given by Hensher, Rose, and Greene (2005):

$$N_m \geq q/(pa^2)\left[\Phi^{-1}(1-\alpha/2)\right]^2 = q/(pa^2)\left[Z_{-1}(1-\alpha/2)\right]^2$$

here $q = 1-p$; $\alpha = 1 - \beta$; and Φ^{-1} is the inverse cumulative distribution function of a standard normal. The allowed deviation from the true population proportion, a, is equivalent to the effect size for sample size calculations

6 Stata's power command has a suite of sample size calculations. A publicly available software, G*Power, can also perform a host of sample size and power calculations.

7 In the following discussion the focus is on determining the sample size for a single-bounded dichotomous choice (SBDC), hence, we will use sample size calculation for proportions. Since the SBDC requires the largest sample size among the contingent valuation models, the sample size calculation discussed in this section serves as the upper bound for CV studies.

8 Rose and Bliemer (2013) refer to these as part of traditional formulas for sample size calculation for discrete choice experiments.

involving tests of means for continuous variables. The term in the brackets is equal to the Z-statistic for a confidence level equal to 1 - $\alpha/2$. Box 3.2 shows an example of how to calculate the sample size using Microsoft Excel®. Based on this formula, the higher the minimum sample size, the lower *p, a,* and α are.

Box 3.2: Calculating the Appropriate Sample Size

As discussed in the text, Hensher, Rose, and Greene (2005) recommend the following formula to calculate the appropriate sample size for a discrete choice experiment. The same formula can be used for a contingent valuation method (CVM) study because a contingent valuation (CV) study is a form of discrete choice experiment wherein the respondent is faced with two alternatives—the status quo versus improved state—presented in a single choice set. To implement the formula for the minimum sample size (N_m), i.e.,

$$N_m \geq q/pa^2\,[\Phi^{-1}\,(1\text{-}\alpha/2)]^2 = q/pa^2\,[Z_{1-\alpha/2})\,]^2$$

the following information is needed:
p – the true population proportion that will choose to support the program, and
a – the allowed error or deviation from the true proportion, expressed as a percentage of the true population proportion p.

Prior information is needed for the values of these parameters. This can come from other related studies that have used the SBDC to value similar hypothetical scenarios in similar institutional and demographic contexts. As discussed in the text this related literature material is gathered as part of the scoping activities for the study. These initial assumptions on the parameters of the formula may be updated based on the results of the pretest of the questionnaire.

For this example, we set p=0.60, that is, 60% of the population will vote or agree to support the program that would lead to changes in the provision of the goods and services. This is equivalent, possibly, to common provision point rule in CV scenarios. The acceptable error or deviation is set at a=0.05 or we allow the range of the true population proportion to be between 55% and 65%. With these assumptions we can compute the minimum sample size using Microsoft Excel®. Implementing the formula requires the use of the inverse standard normal function of Excel or the NORMINV function. Note that as discussed in the text, the result of the NORMINV is the same as the Z-statistic with significance level set at 5%. The result is that the minimum sample size for SBDC under the specific assumptions is 1,024 respondents.

continued on next page

Box 2.5 (continued)

Box Figure 3.1: Results of Sample Size Computation Using Microsoft Excel®

	A	B	C	D	E
1					
2	Alpha	a	1-Alpha/2	Z	sqr Z
3	0.05	0.05	0.975	1.96	3.84
4					
5	True Proportion (p)	q			
6	0.6	0.4			
7					
8	N=	1024			

Box Figure 3.2: Microsoft Excel® Formulas Used in the Sample Size Calculation

	A	B	C	D	E
1					
2	Alpha	a	1-Alpha/2	Z	sqr Z
3	0.05	0.05	=1-A3/2	=NORMINV(C3,0,1)	=D3^2
4					
5	True Proportion (p)	q			
6	0.6	=1-A6			
7					
8	N=	=B6/(A6*(B3^2))*E3			

Source: Authors.

For stratified random sampling, two approaches can be used. The first, when subgroup analysis is not intended, is to compute the sample size for the whole sample, and distribute it across the strata, which can be done in three ways: (i) through equal allocation of the sample size across all strata; (ii) allocating proportional to the size of the strata relative to the population size; and (iii) through optimal allocation which considers both the cost of sampling from each stratum and the desired maximum precision (see Iarossi [2006] for specific cases and formula).

When subgroup analysis is intended, the approach for stratified sampling is to use the formula above to calculate the sample size for each stratum.

The total sample size would just be the sum of the calculated strata level sample sizes. This approach usually results in higher sample sizes.

Other CV studies in the literature have relied either on rules of thumb (Gunatilake et al. 2007; Lauria et al. 2001) or other considerations, apart from minimizing the error of choice proportions of the alternatives (Arrow et al. 1993; Hanemann and Kanninen 2001; Pearce and Ozdemigrolu 2002; Vaughan and Darling 2002; Ao et al. 2016). These recommendations are presented in Table 3.1.

As seen in Table 3.1, the appropriate sample size for a CV study depends on different considerations, including the type of hypothesis that is being tested and the choice of elicitation format. The SBDC format often requires more respondents than the double-bounded dichotomous choice (DBDC) and payment card formats. ADB (2013) cites further practical considerations in determining the sample size.

Table 3.1: Sample Size Recommendations from Selected CVM Studies

Authors	Basis for Sample Size Calculation	Recommended Sample Size
Ao et al. (2016)	Monte Carlo simulations	500 (and 5 bid levels for DBDC)
Arrow et al. (1993)	Sampling error to about ±3%	1,000 (for SBDC)
Gunatilake et al. (2007)	Rule of thumb: CV study had 2 treatments, including 5 bid levels. Computed initial sampling target using 30 respondents per treatment is 300 (30x2x5)	300
Hanemann and Kanninen (2001)	Bias and Variance of Maximum Likelihood Estimator	500–1,000
Lauria et al. (2001)	Rule of thumb: CV study had 30 treatments, including 5 bid levels. Computed initial sampling target using 30 respondents per treatment is 900 (30x30x5). Corrected for proportion of households (60%) with access to water sealed toilets (900/0.60 = 1,500)	1,500
Pearce and Ozdemigrolu (2002)	Sampling error and power of statistical tests	246–1,111
Vaughan and Darling (2002)	Bayesian approach and NPV calculation, which incorporates cost of survey	250–14,000 (depending on cost of survey and desired probability of NPV>0)

CV = contingent valuation, CVM = contingent valuation method, DBDC = double-bounded dichotomous choice, NPV = net present value, SBDC = single-bounded dichotomous choice.
Source: Authors' compilation.

For the payment card elicitation format, since the response or dependent variable is an ordinal approximation of a continuous variable, Mitchell and Carson (1989) suggest the following sample size formula:

$$N_{pc} = 2\,(Z_{1\text{-}\alpha/2} + Z_{1\text{-}\beta})^2\,(V/D)^2$$

This sample size formula is designed to test the hypothesis about the mean WTP (i.e., a null hypothesis for the mean WTP, WTP_0, versus an alternative mean WTP, WTP_1) given a desired effect (D) and power ($Z_{1\text{-}\beta}$) for a single population. This is better than another sample size formula that, for instance, is designed to simply establish a desired confidence interval. The other components of the formula are (i) V which is the coefficient of variation (S_p/WTP$_1$; S_p is the sample standard deviation); and (ii) $Z_{1\text{-}\alpha/2}$ which represents the desired confidence interval. The desired effect D is the percentage difference between the null and alternative WTP means, i.e., WTP_1-WTP_0/WTP_1.

Prior information on V and D is needed to compute the sample size, N_{pc}. Again, this information should be part of the literature review during the scoping activities. Usual assumptions for $Z_{1\text{-}\beta}$ are 0.84 for 80% power and 1.282 for a desired power of 90%. For $Z_{1\text{-}a/2}$, a value of 1.96 is usually used, which represents a significance level of 5% or α =0.05. The prior information or assumptions on the formula parameters can be updated based on the results of the pretest of the initial CV questionnaire, which will be discussed further in Chapter 4.

Survey Mode

The survey is typically administered to the household head through different survey modes. The survey mode is the manner by which the CV questionnaire will be administered or delivered to the respondents. CV surveys can be administered either in person or face-to-face (FTF), sent through the mail, through the telephone, or online (web-based). Each of these modes have advantages and disadvantages in terms of the cost, potential coverage, and response rates. Telephone surveys, for instance, have been a cost-effective mode of survey administration. However, multiple cell phone ownership and call blocking technology have made implementing sampling designs more difficult and have lower response rates (Johnston et al. 2017). The same issues are associated with internet-based surveys. These problems are magnified, especially in the context of a developing country, where access to phone and the internet may be low. Thus, an in-person FTF is sometimes the only possible survey mode in these countries (Whittington 1998). In-person surveys, however, aside from being expensive, are also prone to interviewer effects.

FTF surveys have been greatly aided by technology. The evolution of FTF surveys from pen and paper personal interviews (PAPI) to computer-aided personal interviews (CAPI) has led to a reduction in time and costs while increasing the accuracy of FTF surveys. Furthermore, wages in developing countries are lower than in industrialized countries, making the cost of research personnel also lower. Thus, technology and labor market conditions make FTF survey modes in developing countries more favorable.

In-person interview protocols have also been used to address yea-saying bias in CV studies. For instance, time-to-think (TTT) protocol experiments have been found to result in lower WTP estimates relative to no-time-to-think (or standard in-person) interview estimates (Whittington 2010). TTT protocol involves splitting the interview into two sessions. In the first session, the enumerator completes part of the questionnaire and introduces the CV scenario and questions to the respondent but does not ask for the answers. The response to the CV question is recorded in the second session, thereby giving the respondent time to contemplate or think about the CV scenario overnight. Another survey protocol that has addressed hypothetical bias is the drop-off method (Whittington 2010, citing Subade 2007). The drop-off protocol involves leaving the questionnaire with the respondent overnight and picking it up the following day. Any follow-up question and clarification are made by the enumerator the following day. Like the TTT protocol, the drop-off protocol results in WTP estimates that are 50% lower than the traditional in-person interview.

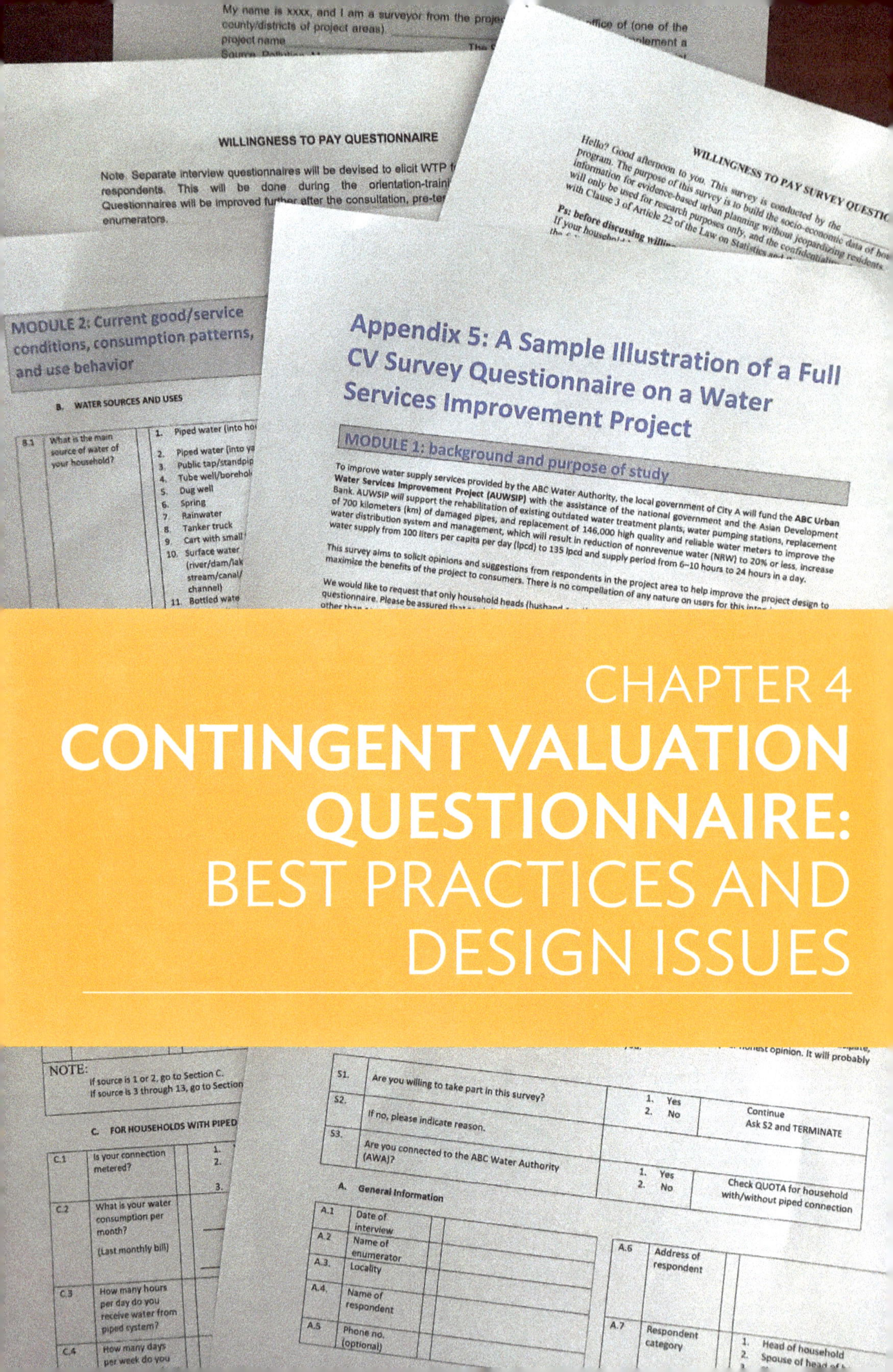

CHAPTER 4

CONTINGENT VALUATION QUESTIONNAIRE: BEST PRACTICES AND DESIGN ISSUES

Key Messages:

- The CV questionnaire is the heart of any CV study.
- The goal of the CV questionnaire is to present a credible hypothetical scenario that respondents will find consequential and will elicit truthful revelation of their willingness to pay for the benefits from the project.
- The different components of the CV questionnaire all contribute to addressing the different biases associated with CVM. Leaving out one component may jeopardize the validity of the CV study.
- The questionnaire should be developed from the point of view of the potential respondents and should be pretested extensively.
- Hypothetical bias is greatly reduced when respondents feel that the changes from the constructed scenario are highly probable and consequential to them.

The CV questionnaire is the heart of a CV study. A well-designed CV survey instrument is characterized as having the basic attributes of being credible, realistic, incentive-compatible, and consequential. An incentive-compatible CV survey design is one that provides adequate incentives for respondents to truthfully reveal their real preference and, hence, the true value of the good or service that is being appraised in their best interest. While consequentiality, on the other hand, is the respondent's belief that the hypothetical scenario is real and that his response will influence the decisions to implement the project and that he will be asked to pay should the project be implemented.

General Structure of a CV Questionnaire

In general, the relevance of the design components of a CV survey depends on how respondents understand and perceive the information presented to them. CV studies that do not follow good survey practices often produce results that are difficult to use and interpret. To ensure that respondents comprehend the CV scenario as intended by the CV team, it should be pretested through focus group discussions and key informant interviews, and contain debriefing questions to check the quality of the information generated.

A typical survey questionnaire should be designed to fit the study context and generally contains modules and suggested content, as described in Table 4.1.

Table 4.1: Modules and Contents of a CV Questionnaire

Module	Description	Content
Module 1	Introductory Module	Brief background of the subject; confidentiality and informed consent; household identification numbers; cluster identification (if cluster sampling was used); contact details for follow-up information (if need arises)
Module 2	Knowledge, Attitudes, and Behavioral Questions	Includes questions that gauges the respondent's knowledge and perceptions related to the existing attributes of the good and services being valued, institutions tasked to deliver these goods and services, importance of proposed changes, other issues related to the goods and services being valued, etc. Activities and other actions related to the goods and services (e.g., defensive measures against water pollution like boiling water, health and other expenditures, consumption patterns, etc.)
Module 3	CV Scenario Module	Description of hypothetical market; attributes of the good and services that are relevant to respondents; changes in levels of attributes with and without the project; valuation question and elicitation format; payment vehicle; and debriefing questions (see section 4.2 for more detailed discussions)
Module 4	Demographic and Socioeconomic Profile Module	Household size, age, gender, education, occupation, number of income earners, asset ownership, income levels, and expenditure pattern

Source: Authors.

The Contingent Valuation Scenario

The CV scenario is arguably the most important part of a CV questionnaire. It typically includes a description of three important elements: (i) the project or program or policy/change of interest, (ii) the constructed market, and (iii) the method of payment. Johnston et al. (2017) summarized the design issues mentioned by various studies and listed some important considerations when designing a CV scenario, which include (i) respondents' prior experience and knowledge of the good being valued; (ii) framing of the valuation questions in the questionnaire; (iii) completeness of information in the questionnaire that can affect a respondent's response to the valuation questions (i.e., payment mechanisms, institutional arrangements, etc.); and the (iv) sequencing or order of valuation questions. In general, proper design and framing of the hypothetical CV scenario can lead to accurate and reliable WTP estimates, which are usually contingent on these elements. As highlighted in Table 2.4 a good CV scenario also mitigates the major behavioral biases found in CVM studies (e.g., hypothetical and strategic bias).

The next section discusses in detail the components of the CV scenario modules and the current best practices underlying their construction.

Description of the Changes in the Good or Benefits to Be Valued

The attributes of the good or service being valued should be described in a clear and simple manner so that respondents can easily understand and make proper judgments. The scenario must have a well-defined description of a reference level (without-project scenario) compared with a target level (state of the world with the proposed change or the "with-project scenario") of each attribute of interest. Vague qualitative scales such as "high," "medium," and "low" in describing changes must be avoided unless these are clearly defined for and understood by respondents (Johnston et al. 2017). Respondents should be able to establish a clear link between intermediate changes and "final" changes that directly affect their well-being. This will help them recognize how intermediate changes can impact their welfare (Boyd and Krupnick 2009; Boyd et al. 2016; Johnston et al. 2017). Box 4.1 shows an example of how a CV scenario defines the "change" in a good or service being valued in a water supply improvement project.

Box 4.1: Defining the Change in the Good or Service Being Valued

The changes in the provision of the good or service should be presented clearly so that respondents understand them. The example below shows an excerpt of the contingent valuation (CV) scenario in Gunatilake and Tachirii (2014). Their study looks at the willingness to pay for improved water supply services in urban Bangladesh.

CV scenario excerpt:

> "The proposed project will involve sourcing raw water from the river to meet the water demand of households and business enterprises. Water will be treated to make it **safe for human consumption**. This means sufficient water will be made available to the household, water will be **safe to drink from the tap**, and therefore will **not need boiling, filtering, or treating.** Water will be **available 24 hours a day with sufficient water pressure, so there would be no need to store water.**"

The changes are clear and are phrased in nontechnical language. This scenario was informed by extensive engagements and pretesting with relevant stakeholders.

Source: Authors.

Johnston et al. (2017) noted that valuation scenarios, which may involve spatial and temporal changes, or some risk or uncertainty as an important feature of the valuation,[9] should be communicated to the respondents. Researchers must look for pieces of evidence that the valuation scenario is understood, accepted, and perceived as credible by respondents to enable an accurate expectation of its likely effect on their well-being. This evidence is often gleaned during the pretesting of the questionnaire. Hypothetical bias is greatly reduced when respondents feel that the changes from the constructed scenario are highly probable and consequential to them.

Description of the Constructed Market

One of the key elements of the constructed market is the technical and political feasibility of the change. For instance, is the water service provider willing and able to deliver the proposed water service improvements? Is it in their mandate to provide sewerage services? Another important element is the conditionality of providing the good. If respondents believe that the provision of the good is conditional on how much they are willing to pay, then they are likely to engage in strategic behavior to influence its provision (Mitchell and Carson 1989). Also, the timing of provision, which refers to when and for how long the good will be provided, must be defined explicitly.

The Payment Vehicle

The payment vehicle refers to the mechanism used to collect money from households or tourists to finance the hypothetical provision of the good. The "payment vehicle" could either be voluntary or mandatory. Voluntary payments include donations and gifts while mandatory contributions include taxes, utility bills, entrance fees, and charges, among others. Table 4.2 shows some of the payment vehicles that are used in different sectors.

Choosing an appropriate payment vehicle is relevant to a CV study because it ultimately affects WTP estimates, as respondents tend to engage in strategic behavior when faced with different modes of payment. Strategic behavior induced by inappropriate payment vehicle choice leads to payment vehicle bias. For instance, respondents tend to exaggerate their

[9] The researcher should also consider the objective information and the respondents' subjective view of this information. Also, the guidelines noted the need to identify the "temporal, spatial, uncertainty, and risk dimensions, and whether the baseline and change(s) are individual or household-specific" (Johnston et al. 2017).

WTP when payment is voluntary, while a compulsory payment could also provide them with an incentive to give a low WTP.

Table 4.2: Examples of Payment Vehicles

Sector	Payment Vehicle
Water and wastewater	Water bill, annual tax (i.e., business tax)
Biodiversity conservation	Donations or contribution to a special fund, utility bill (water and electricity), income tax
Energy	Electricity bill, tax, contribution to a special fund
Tourism	Entrance fee, environmental fee, one-time donation, or contribution to a special fund
Solid waste	Annual tax (i.e., land/building tax, business tax), monthly charge (i.e., garbage fee)

Source: Authors.

The choice of a payment vehicle will ultimately depend on the good being valued and the context in which it is to be provided. While there is no consensus on a specific payment vehicle, there are some criteria to help evaluate the choice of a suitable payment mechanism:

- Inclusive/universal – everybody will be made to pay (i.e., electricity bill).
- Credible – use of incentive-compatible payment methods that are binding (fixed and nonmalleable) to minimize the risk of strategic behavior and prevent free-riding.
- Relevant – likely to be employed in the real-world decision, i.e., surcharge for water service and sewerage improvements can be collected through a water bill.
- Acceptable – there is no strong aversion to the payment mechanism.

It is also important to choose a neutral payment vehicle so that it does not influence the respondent's valuation of the good. For instance, valuing a public good using referendum voting may require payment mechanisms such as taxes or a utility surcharge. However, this may elicit a strong dislike from respondents who may object to the principle of paying for the good through higher taxes or utility rates (Georgiou et al. 1998). This may be due to mistrust of a collecting agency. They may then reject the program not because they have no preference for the good but rather as an act of protest against the collecting agency. In such cases, another credible payment vehicle may be considered.

Meanwhile, voluntary contributions are often not recommended. Voluntary payments provide a strong incentive for respondents to engage in strategic behavior,[10] leading them to misstate their true valuation of the good (Carson, Groves, and Machina 1999; Champ et al. 2002). Respondents may overestimate their WTP to obtain the provision of the good with an option to forgo future contributions. Nonetheless, there may be unavoidable context-specific cases where voluntary and other nonbinding payment mechanisms are necessary. In such cases, corrective bias mechanisms such as including provision point mechanisms in the decision rule (see discussion on decision rule or provision point mechanism) could potentially improve welfare estimates (Alston and Nowell 1996; Rondeau, Schulze, and Poe 1999; Poe et al. 2002; Rose et al. 2002). As discussed in the following section, the inclusion of a provision point mechanism to the voluntary payment scenario could improve WTP estimates compared with a purely voluntary payment script (Champ et al. 2002).

Other features of the payment vehicle, such as who pays (e.g., household, or individual), duration/timing of payment (e.g., lump sum/one-time versus periodic), and frequency of payment (annual or monthly) must be context specific as well as credible and relevant to the respondents. It must also cover an adequate proportion of the population so that results can be aggregated to the general population. If, for instance, the chosen payment vehicle is potentially applicable to a few people in the population then the WTP derived from a sample cannot realistically be aggregated to the larger population.

Initial Bid Range and Levels[11]

Once the payment vehicle has been chosen the initial range and level of payments or bids should be determined. The literature review during the scoping activities (see discussion in Chapter 2) should already give an idea on the likely range (i.e., minimum and maximum value) of people's willingness to pay for the good or service that is being valued. Of course, inflation and currency exchange adjustments should be made when obtaining information from studies of a different period and/or country. In the absence

[10] Respondents tend to overstate their responses if stated WTP is perceived to be unrelated to actual payment since it increases the chance that the good will be provided without them having to pay for it (free riding). The alternate is also true—respondents could understate their WTP if they know that actual contributions will be made.

[11] The process described in this section is called the naïve process. More sophisticated methods of choosing the bid range and levels are discussed in Kim and Haab (2004).

of similar related literature, the initial range can be obtained by asking focus group respondents or key informants for their maximum and minimum willingness to pay for the hypothetical changes. This can be done during the qualitative pretesting of the questionnaire which will be discussed further in the next chapter.

When the range of payment has been decided, the bid levels (i.e., the payment levels between the minimum and maximum bids or payments) need to be chosen. Carson and Hanemann (2005) citing Alberini and Carson (1990) recommend between 4 and 8 bid levels including the minimum and maximum bids. The common practice is to distribute the bid levels equally (i.e., equidistant between the minimum and maximum bid range). This initial bid range and levels need to be pretested and recalibrated as discussed in the next chapter .

The Elicitation Format

After all the elements of the CV scenario have been properly defined, the next step is to frame the valuation question to determine how much respondents would be willing to pay for the good under a given decision rule. In CV practice, the prices stated by respondents in reply to the question are referred to as bids.

Researchers need to consider the potential advantages and disadvantages of each elicitation method (an overview of the methods is provided in Chapter 2), especially the differences in its incentive properties (Harrison 2006; Carson and Groves 2007; Carson, Chilton, and Hutchinson 2009; Carson, Groves, and List 2014). For valuing public goods, and private goods sold in controlled markets, the single dichotomous choice (SBDC) response format is often considered to achieve better incentive compatibility than other elicitation formats (Carson and Groves 2007; Cummings, Harrison and Rutström 1995; Cummings et al. 1997; Carson, Groves, and Machina 1999; Johnston et al. 2017; List 2014; Pattanayak et al. 2006).

In comparison, open-ended questions yield either unrealistically high or frequent zero WTP responses rendering them non-incentive compatible and prone to strategic behavior (Carson and Groves 2007). The iterative-bidding question format may be susceptible to anchoring effects while payment cards may suffer from range effects.

The SBDC formats, however, are not universally superior. They may also be associated with bid anchoring, although these concerns can be mitigated with appropriate survey design and pretesting (Johnston et al. 2017). SBDC in a referendum voting format has been found to be less applicable in context where there is less familiarity with democratic processes (Zhongmin et al. 2003). To randomize bid amounts, SBDC also requires customized questionnaires per respondent, and thus precise enumeration control by economists, in addition to demanding larger sample sizes than other options. It may also not be amenable to adjusting WTP in case of differences between sample and beneficiary characteristics. This suggests that while SBDC is often preferrable for its incentive compatibility properties, use of other elicitation formats may be more appropriate in specific circumstances.

Decision Rule or Provision Point Mechanism

The decision rule or provision point mechanism is another CV design feature that addresses the issue of strategic bias and the related free-riding behavior. Under this mechanism, the good will only be provided if certain conditions are met. Currently, common provision point mechanisms are used depending on whether payments are mandatory or voluntary. In the mandatory payment format, the provision point mechanism is combined with a referendum vote format and takes the form of a majority vote. In this case, the respondent is told that the good will be provided if 60% of households will vote for its provision in a referendum. For voluntary payment vehicles such as charitable donations, on the other hand, the provision point mechanism comes in the form of meeting a lower bound threshold combined with a payback guarantee in the CV scenario. For example, if 60% of the funding requirement is not met through voluntary contributions, the program will not push through, and the respondents will be reimbursed for their contributions.

Arrow et al. (1993) recommended that valuation questions must be framed as a referendum vote[12] under the context of a majority rule. However, Johnston et al. (2017) noted that this recommendation was directed toward the estimation of nonuse values for public goods in the United States and, thus, may be inapplicable or unrealistic in a nondemocratic political setting

[12] A referendum is a general vote by the electorate on a single political question that has been referred to them for a direct decision. Using this format in a CV study, respondents are asked to vote yes or no to a single-bounded dichotomous choice CV question for a proposed project or policy that will bring about changes in nonmarketed goods.

or where public good provision is not determined through a referendum. Hence, a referendum format under a majority voting mechanism should only be considered where it is feasible. In nondemocratic countries where referenda are not conducted, other binding and credible public decision-making processes should be considered.

There are also cases where referendum votes may not apply, such as in recreation choices and private goods. It is unrealistic to offer a tourist from elsewhere in the country, for instance, a scenario wherein she would be voting in a local referendum. In general, the choice of a decision rule or provision point mechanism should be one that is plausible and binding for all respondents (Johnston et al. 2017). Furthermore, the use of provision point mechanisms to address strategic bias has yielded mixed results, leading most studies to concur that this correction method needs further investigation, especially when applied to voluntary contributions[13] (Champ et al. 2002; Groothuis and Whitehead 2009; Christantoni and Damigos 2018).

Cheap Talk and Reminders of Substitutes and Income Constraints

The "cheap talk" approach is also one of the hypothetical bias mitigation tools applied to CV studies (Cummings and Taylor 1999; Lusk 2003). Originally used in experimental economics, cheap talk is essentially a script that contains several reminders before the respondent makes a choice in the context of the hypothetical scenario. An important component of the script is a reminder to respondents of the hypothetical nature of CV scenarios and the general observed tendency to overstate value estimates under this condition. The National Oceanic and Atmospheric Administration (NOAA) panel earlier also recommended direct reminders of the presence of substitute goods[14] and the individual's budget constraint[15] (i.e., paying for the good means forgoing other expenses) in the CV scenario. Stated explicitly in a non-neutral manner, these reminders will help respondents weigh comparable alternatives to the good being valued when making decisions.

---

[13] Specifically, while experimental economics suggest that the provision point mechanism (PPM) is effective in eliminating free-riding behavior by providing incentives to respondents to truthfully reveal their preferences, some CV studies dealing with voluntary donations show otherwise. Groothuis and Whitehead (2009) noted that PPM under a voluntary context may lead to scenario rejection especially at higher bid prices, thereby leading to a downward bias in willingness-to-pay estimates.

[14] This reminds respondents that the good being valued may not be unique, which has implications on its value.

[15] Given their limited income, respondents are reminded of the need to trade off money for the good or service being valued.

Many studies validate the observation that cheap talk reduces or eliminates hypothetical bias[16] (Lusk 2003; Murphy, Stevens, and Weatherhead 2005; Landry and List 2007; Champ, Moore, and Bishop 2009) although it does so more effectively in the traditional referendum than in a voluntary format. However, certain conditions may limit the robustness of cheap talk as a bias correction approach, such as for example (i) the respondents' prior experience or knowledge of the good being valued (List 2001; Lusk 2003; Champ, Moore, and Bishop 2009); (ii) use of a concise and neutral script (Aadland and Caplan 2006); and (iii) where monetary consequences of decisions or payment amounts are small (Brown et al. 2003; Murphy, Stevens, and Weatherhead 2005). On the other hand, studies on reminders of substitutes and budget constraints have shown that while the information does not affect mean willingness to pay, it tends to improve the precision of WTP estimates (Loomis, Gonzalez-Caban, and Gregory 1994; Kotchen and Reiling 2000).

These findings provide further guidance on when to use the cheap talk script and how it is best designed. When the bid amounts are very small, and the respondents are very familiar with the good or service being valued then the benefits from a cheap talk script may be outweighed by the cognitive and time costs borne by the respondent from a longer questionnaire. Reminders that substitutes and income constraints have a neutral effect on WTP can be part of the CV scenario regardless of the bid values and the level of the respondent's familiarity with the good.

Unlike cheap talk, cognitive dissonance minimization or oath taking is a relatively new ex-ante mitigation tool that is also increasingly being used to reduce hypothetical bias. Respondents are requested to sign an oath stating that they agree to honestly state their true value for the good when responding to the valuation question (Ehmke et al. 2008). CV studies that investigated the effect of an oath script in different countries indicate that in some cases, an oath script can lower the respondent's mean willingness to pay while also leading to lower variances (Jacquemet et al. 2009; Morrison and Brown 2009; Stevens, Tabatabaei, and Lass 2013; Hanxiao and Botao 2019). However, De-Magistris et al. (2016) pointed out in their result that oath scripts can only effectively reduce hypothetical bias for people with high educational attainment.

[16] WTP estimates with a cheap talk script are significantly lower than those in the hypothetical survey without the cheap talk script.

In comparing cheap talk with oath scripts, Jacquemet et al. (2009, p. 33) concluded, "while cheap talk helps truthful people bid in better accordance with their true preferences, it is the oath that increases the odds of truthfulness in the sample." However, given the mixed results of entreaties as a mechanism to reduce hypothetical bias from CV studies, Johnston et al. (2017) cautioned that the incentive properties of these methods are not yet clear, including the means through which they influence behavior. Its applicability in developing countries may also be limited as it might violate local cultural norms. Hence, these methods need to be investigated further, especially their application in developing countries.

Debriefing and Follow-Up Questions

Debriefing questions are designed ex ante to evaluate the validity of responses to the valuation question. Hence, these must be pretested to ensure that they meet their intended purpose (Krupnick and Adamowicz 2006). These include identifying protest responses or other motivations for the valuation response by asking respondents why they chose to say "yes" or "no" to the price or bid for the proposed outcome. Another purpose is to determine whether respondents understand, believe, or accept the information given in the valuation scenario, such as the payment mechanism and other institutional factors that influence the provision of the good or service (Krupnick and Adamowicz 2006; Ivehammar 2009). Debriefing questions can also help evaluate how respondents perceive the survey instrument in terms of its consequentiality, neutrality, and level of difficulty, among others (Johnston et al. 2017). Excessive protest and scenario rejection, which are captured in these debriefing and follow-up questions, are grounds to doubt the validity of the CV study.

Uncertainty Correction

Cummings and Taylor (1999) introduced the use of a follow-up certainty question to reduce the effect of hypothetical bias manifested through "yea-saying" behavior. Yea-saying behavior is the tendency of respondents to agree to an offered bid either because they find the hypothetical scenario difficult to comprehend or feel that the scenario is inconsequential to them. Using a Likert scale, respondents are probed on how sure they are to say "yes" to the valuation question. Those who said "yes" to the valuation question but are uncertain of their answer are recorded as negative (or no) responses. CV studies that included a certainty follow-up question have been consistently shown to mitigate hypothetical bias, resulting in a mean

WTP that is not significantly different from the actual payment treatment (Champ et al. 1997; Johannesson et al. 1999; Blumenschein et al. 2008). Some studies have shown that a follow-up certainty approach is more consistent than the cheap talk approach in eliminating hypothetical bias (Little and Berrens 2004; Blumenschein et al. 2008; Champ, Moore, and Bishop 2009; Morrison and Brown 2009).

Protest Correction

Another method to correct payment vehicle bias as well as other potential sources of bias in the CV scenario is to identify protest responses. A protest response typically happens when a respondent does not provide their "true" willingness to pay for the good and instead states a zero value or a "protest response" (Mitchell and Carson 1989). The respondent rejects paying for the good not because he or she does not value it but because he or she may dislike some elements in the CV scenario, such as the payment mechanism or uncertainty, or may be skeptical that the good will be provided. Another reason for the protest behavior is that the respondent feels that he or she has property rights over the changes a project, policy, or program creates. Thus, asking him or her to pay for these changes leads to a rejection of the CV scenario.

Protest behavior is identified by asking the respondent a follow-up or debriefing question as to his or her reason for not supporting the program or choosing a certain payment level. The common approach in dealing with protest zeros is to drop them from the sample or include a covariate to control for the behavior. However, when there is a significant number of protest responses, such an approach may greatly reduce the sample size and compromise data efficiency and bias welfare estimates. Thus, effects on the regression estimates should be observed when protest correction is done.

Other Follow-Up Questions

Aside from debriefing questions that account for protest and uncertainty, follow-up questions should probe for the respondents' understanding of the scenario and their perceptions of its consequentiality—such as the promised changes, the institutional setup that will deliver the change, and the payment vehicle. Poor understanding or skepticism of these elements usually indicate scenario rejection. Consequentiality questions, on the other hand, should reveal the respondents' perception on whether the actual results of the study will be used and lead to the promised changes. Respondents who do not feel strongly that the results of the study will be of consequence to policy makers are often also dropped from the analysis.

An Annotated Example of a CV Scenario Module

In this section, an annotated example of a CV scenario module for a water improvement project is presented. This example covers all the elements discussed in the earlier sections, to help the reader visualize a CV scenario module that follows the current preferred best practices. The annotations are included to provide brief motivations for each element as discussed in detail in the previous sections. Figure 4.1 shows the annotated CV scenario module. Appendix 4, on the other hand, presents a different CV scenario module for water supply improvement resulting from a forest conservation project that also conforms to good practices in CV scenario design.

Figure 4.1: An Annotated Example of a CV Scenario Module

A. Current Context and Problems

The ABC Water Authority (AWA) is mandated to develop and regulate water supply and wastewater. In particular, 70% of households in City A and City B pay water tariffs for their metered connections, thereby, contributing to the bulk of AWA's revenues. However, in recent years, its level of service has been deteriorating with intermittent and inequitable water supply and areas with low water pressure due to lack of maintenance and improvement, i.e., rehabilitation of assets. Leakages in the water distribution pipelines are 10 times the accepted norm, with approximately half of them needing replacement. Nonrevenue water (NRW) from technical losses has steadily increased up to more than 50%.

The leakages in the pipelines are putting an increasing maintenance burden on AWA, particularly in fixing the leaks. As a result of the large NRW in the water distribution networks, all water treatment plants (WTPs) servicing both cities are challenged by the demand for higher volume of water. Most WTPs are currently operating above their design capacity including most of their pump stations. The latter has been operating inefficiently and unreliably because of the steady and increasing backlog in capital maintenance, which needs urgent intervention. The WTPs are also using techniques and processes that do not meet the national drinking water quality standards introduced in 2012. Consequently, the deteriorating quality of tap water in households has been increasing risk to public health.

B. The ABC Urban Water Services Improvement Project and Its Benefits

To address these problems, the Government of ABC (GOA) through the AWA Division of City A is planning to implement the ABC Urban Water Services Improvement Project (AUWSIP). The proposed AUWSIP will support water supply improvement in City A through (i) improvement in the efficiency of water distribution network in City A, (ii) repair and upgrading of water treatment plants to meet the national drinking water standards, (iii) rehabilitation of water pumping stations in City A and City B to improve efficiency, and (iv) upgrading of institutional capacity to support the proposed interventions and to ensure sustainable benefits.

Let me now discuss the notable benefits and changes the project will achieve [enumerator shows Card A and reads through].

Once the program is implemented, households connected to the new water distribution network will experience an improvement in the quality of piped water. In particular, the tap water will no longer taste and smell bad, and households can now drink directly from the tap. This would save time and costs because tap water will no longer need to be boiled for drinking. There will be adequate water pressure, which would allow households like you to use several faucets simultaneously. Currently, using several faucets at the same time results in low water pressure; causing only a trickle of water out of the faucet. Other household members usually need to wait while one member uses the faucet.

This part of the CV Module should include the context of the policy or project, the institutions that will be involved, and a layman's description of the project activities or components that will deliver the proposed changes in the good or service that will be valued.

In the case of ADB, this information is often found in pre-project documents or inception reports. Information from these documents can be used in initial drafts of the questionnaire, but subsequent verification through focus group discussions (FGDs) and questionnaire pretesting should also be done.

This describes the changes in the attributes of the good or service that the project, program, or policy will create. In this example, the good is improved water quality defined as a set of attributes or characteristics. It explicitly describes the changes between the levels of each attribute in without the project and with the project scenarios. The intent is to provide the respondent with precise information on what exactly is he/she is paying for or valuing.

Thus, broad and vague phrases such as "the project will improve water quality" should be avoided.

continued...

continued on next page

Figure 4.1 (continued)

The project would eliminate the need for household members to wait for each other when using the faucet. Water will also be available 24 hours a day and 7 days a week in contrast with current water availability at 6 to 10 hours a day. The project will also expand connection to include the most vulnerable and poor households in these cities. It would also benefit AWA by reducing their losses from nonrevenue water from 50% to only 20%.

... continued

Broad and vague phrases make it hard for the respondent to visualize the change the project will create and, therefore, reduces the consequentiality of the CV scenario.

Card A: Benefits and Changes

Attribute	Without the Project Level (Without AUWSIP)	With the Project Level (or After AUWSIP Completion)
Water potability	Cannot drink directly from the tap; need to boil water	Can drink directly from the tap
Water taste	Tastes bad	Tastes sweet or good
Water odor	Smells bad	No smell
Water availability	Water available 6–10 hours/day	Water available 24x7
Water pressure	Cannot use all faucets simultaneously and only one faucet can be used at a time	All faucets in the house can be turned on simultaneously
Supply to vulnerable households	No supply	100%
Nonrevenue water	50%	20%

Level descriptions can either be qualitative or quantitative. This would depend on how the respondents understand and perceive these levels. Pretesting of the questionnaire is a must.

Use of visual aids such as summary tables, videos, pictures, and other multimedia platforms are very effective in helping respondents understand what he/she is actually valuing or paying for. It is highly advisable to utilize visual aids.

Improving the water supply system and its delivery through the activities mentioned above will require funds. With a limited budget available, the government will either reallocate funds from other expenditure items or increase the tariff. In the former case, the government could compromise other development expenditures in favor of the water supply development. Hence, another viable option would be to rationalize the water tariff and adopt a ring-fenced accounting system so that AWA utilizes the tariff revenue solely for the purpose of the improvement, maintenance, and upkeep of the water supply intervention.

C. CV Question and Referendum

Suppose that the AWA Division of City A decides to push through with the AUWSIP through a referendum. The project will only be implemented if 60% of households will vote for it. But with the completion and implementation of the project, people would have to pay higher water bills. If you vote against the plan, your water bills would not increase, but the water service and quality will not improve either.

This sentence is called a "**provision point rule or mechanism.**" It indicates the condition or rule that when satisfied will lead to the improvement in water quality. It is a bias-reducing mechanism. In particular, it reduces the potential free-riding behavior.

This survey is only meant to get your opinion on whether you would decide to vote for the AUWSIP if it is implemented in your area. Past studies show that people say YES when asked of their opinion in a survey, but they would vote NO in a real situation. Researchers are not sure why they do this. It could be because it feels good to say yes in a survey when you do not actually have to pay. Or it could be to please the person doing the interview. However, please try to tell us how you would answer in an actual situation. Please say yes only

These paragraphs comprise the "**cheap talk script.**" Cheap talk is a bias-reducing mechanism that reduces "yea-saying" behavior. This behavior is known to inflate WTP estimates. The script contains (i) a description of what hypothetical bias is, and

continued...

continued on next page

Figure 4.1 (continued)

if you are really willing to support the plan to improve the water quality services in your city.

Also please consider your household's capacity to pay. Payment for these improvements means forgoing other household expenditures.

Different households also have different water consumption and expenditures. The average household with five members consumes around 25 cubic meters (m^3) of water per month and pays ₱175/household (hh)/month. You may not be one of the average households and may have a higher or lower consumption and bill than average. But I would like you to think as if you are an average household consuming and paying this average amount per month.

Would you vote for the AUWSIP if it means that you and your family will have to pay an additional amount of ____₱/hh/month to be added to your monthly water bill for improved water quality and services?

1. **Yes (Go to D.1.A)**
2. **No (Go to D.1.C)**

... continued

(ii) a reminder of budget constraint and opportunity cost of an affirmative vote.

This paragraph is called the **"hypothetical baseline."** This provides a common reference or starting point for all respondents.

This is the contingent valuation question. It is phrased as a "voting referendum." The elicitation format is called a single-bound dichotomous choice (SBDC). Note also that it is phrased as a behavioral intent question and not as a willingness-to-pay question (i.e., *"Are you willing to pay ...?"*). Behavioral intent questions are easier to compare with actual behavior and are less speculative (Whitehead 2006). A straight WTP question asks what a respondent will pay for something rather than what they would do in a certain situation.

D. Debriefing Questions

Debriefing questions are a set of questions whose goal is to understand the respondent's answers and perceptions on the CV scenario.

D.1. Reasons for the Referendum Vote

D.1.A. If yes, how sure are you that you would pay?

1. Very unsure
2. Unsure
3. Sure
4. Very sure

The answer to this question allows for uncertainty correction. "Yes" votes are converted to "No" if the respondent is either unsure or very unsure of his/her vote. Uncertainty correction also mitigates the effect of "yea-saying" behavior.

D.1.B. Why did you agree to support the plan? *(choose one or more options, as applicable)*

1. I am using the water services, therefore I should pay
2. I want to abide by the law
3. Quality and quantity of water will improve
4. The project will benefit a lot of people
5. It makes me feel good just knowing I am part of a noble initiative
6. Others, pls specify: ______________________

(Go to D.1.D)

D.1.C. What is the main reason why you did not vote to support the plan? *(choose one option)*

1. I cannot afford the additional monthly fee
2. I am not sure about the sustainability of the plan
3. I don't like the additional charges to be added to my water bill
4. I don't like AWA managing the construction and operation of the project
5. I don't see the need for rehabilitation of pipelines and water treatment plants
6. It is the government's responsibility, not mine, to pay for the project
7. Others, pls specify: ______________

The objective of the question is to qualify whether "no" votes are protest votes or not. Respondents exhibiting protest behavior are dropped from the sample. Thus, the answer to this question facilitates protest correction.

continued on next page

Figure 4.1 (continued)

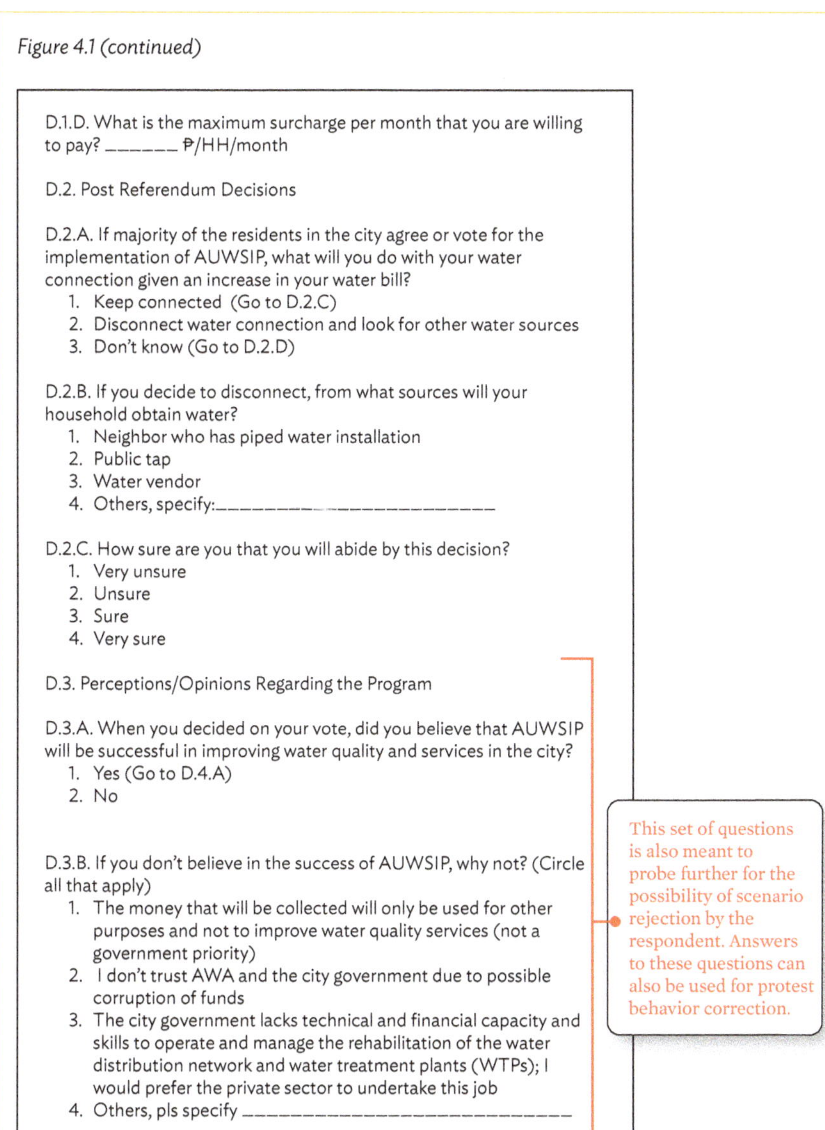

D.1.D. What is the maximum surcharge per month that you are willing to pay? ______ ₱/HH/month

D.2. Post Referendum Decisions

D.2.A. If majority of the residents in the city agree or vote for the implementation of AUWSIP, what will you do with your water connection given an increase in your water bill?
1. Keep connected (Go to D.2.C)
2. Disconnect water connection and look for other water sources
3. Don't know (Go to D.2.D)

D.2.B. If you decide to disconnect, from what sources will your household obtain water?
1. Neighbor who has piped water installation
2. Public tap
3. Water vendor
4. Others, specify:____________________________

D.2.C. How sure are you that you will abide by this decision?
1. Very unsure
2. Unsure
3. Sure
4. Very sure

D.3. Perceptions/Opinions Regarding the Program

D.3.A. When you decided on your vote, did you believe that AUWSIP will be successful in improving water quality and services in the city?
1. Yes (Go to D.4.A)
2. No

D.3.B. If you don't believe in the success of AUWSIP, why not? (Circle all that apply)
1. The money that will be collected will only be used for other purposes and not to improve water quality services (not a government priority)
2. I don't trust AWA and the city government due to possible corruption of funds
3. The city government lacks technical and financial capacity and skills to operate and manage the rehabilitation of the water distribution network and water treatment plants (WTPs); I would prefer the private sector to undertake this job
4. Others, pls specify ____________________________
____

This set of questions is also meant to probe further for the possibility of scenario rejection by the respondent. Answers to these questions can also be used for protest behavior correction.

continued on next page

Figure 4.1 (continued)

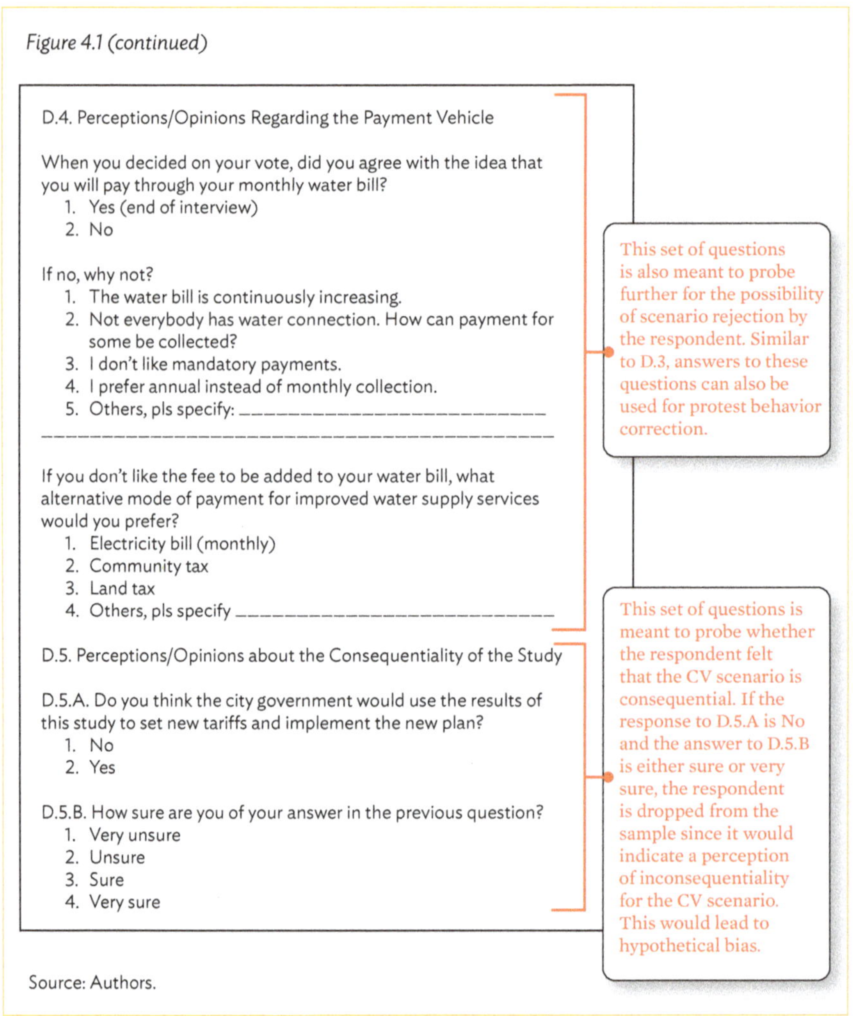
D.4. Perceptions/Opinions Regarding the Payment Vehicle

When you decided on your vote, did you agree with the idea that you will pay through your monthly water bill?
1. Yes (end of interview)
2. No

If no, why not?
1. The water bill is continuously increasing.
2. Not everybody has water connection. How can payment for some be collected?
3. I don't like mandatory payments.
4. I prefer annual instead of monthly collection.
5. Others, pls specify: ____________________________
____

If you don't like the fee to be added to your water bill, what alternative mode of payment for improved water supply services would you prefer?
1. Electricity bill (monthly)
2. Community tax
3. Land tax
4. Others, pls specify ____________________________

D.5. Perceptions/Opinions about the Consequentiality of the Study

D.5.A. Do you think the city government would use the results of this study to set new tariffs and implement the new plan?
1. No
2. Yes

D.5.B. How sure are you of your answer in the previous question?
1. Very unsure
2. Unsure
3. Sure
4. Very sure

This set of questions is also meant to probe further for the possibility of scenario rejection by the respondent. Similar to D.3, answers to these questions can also be used for protest behavior correction.
This set of questions is meant to probe whether the respondent felt that the CV scenario is consequential. If the response to D.5.A is No and the answer to D.5.B is either sure or very sure, the respondent is dropped from the sample since it would indicate a perception of inconsequentiality for the CV scenario. This would lead to hypothetical bias.

Source: Authors.

Auxiliary Questions: Warm-Up, Behavioral, and Demographic Questions

While the CV scenario module is the heart of the CV questionnaire, there are other supplementary questions that are important to include, such as the respondents' attitudes, opinions, behavior, knowledge, and experiences about the good being valued. Usually considered neutral and nonthreatening, these supplementary questions or "warm-up" questions are typically placed at the beginning of the questionnaire (referred to as modules 1 and 2 in Table 4.1). They engage respondents to respond to a broader set of topics before leading them to the specific valuation scenario. On the other hand, it is recommended that auxiliary questions are placed at the end of the questionnaire to keep interest and attention of the respondents focused on the CV questions rather than questions that are easier to answer. Appendix 5 provides an example of a complete CV survey questionnaire on a water improvement project.

Covariates used in subsequent regression models are taken from a subset of these auxiliary questions, such as income, age, education, gender, attitude, and knowledge questions. They help explain the responses to the valuation question and can enable estimates to be transferred to the beneficiary population if the sample is not fully representative. Hence, the survey team must collect relevant covariates through rigorous pretesting. Otherwise, it will not be possible to logically interpret valuation responses.

When formulating knowledge, attitude, and perception questions, a researcher can consider related studies as well as relevant information obtained from focus group discussions and personal interviews. Box 4.2 shows an example of how a conceived behavioral model can be used to organize the flow or sequence of questions in the questionnaire.

Box 4.2: Using Behavioral Models to Organize the Flow or Sequence of Questions

In the case of a sewerage or septage project, several questions can be asked, such as *Do you have a toilet? Why or why not? Does your toilet have a septic tank? When and how frequently do you desludge your septic tank?* A behavioral model can be used to design these series of questions coherently. One such model posits that sanitation decision-making occurs in stages or as ladders of behavior. This decision-making process could and should be reflected in the design of the flow/order of questions. A screener question can help divide the stages of behavior or decision into subsections. Following this behavioral model can lead to a better structured, more coherent, and well-organized sequence of questions that will also help enumerators administer the questionnaire effectively to respondents. The box figure provides an example of how to organize behavioral questions about water, wastewater, and sanitation behavior based on a specific behavioral model.

Flow of Behavioral Questions

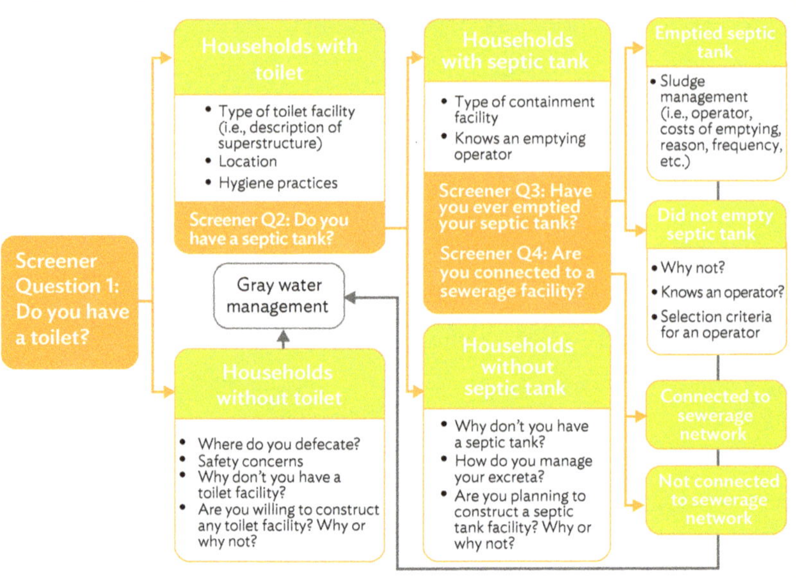

Source: Authors.

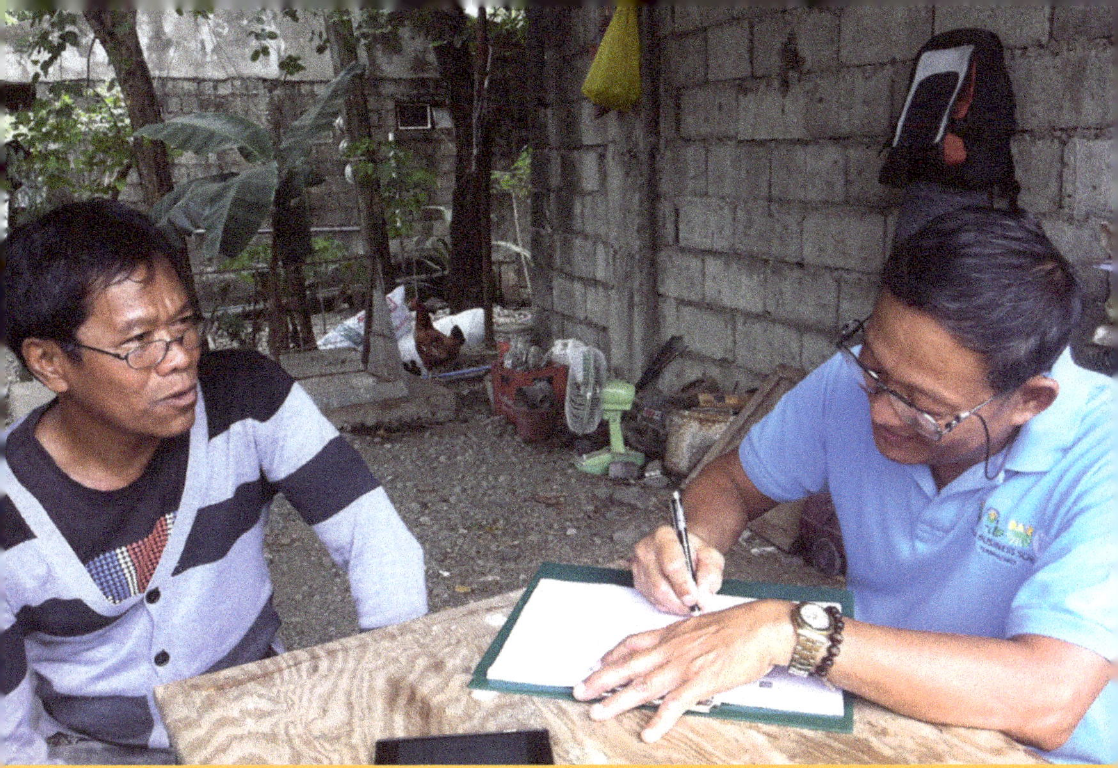

CHAPTER 5

IMPLEMENTATION OF CONTINGENT VALUATION SURVEYS

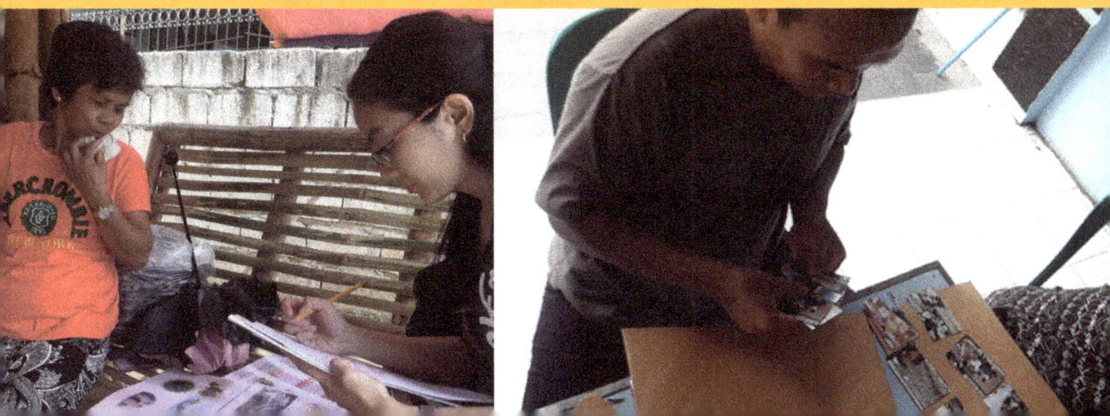

Key Messages:

- Contingent valuation surveys follow common good practices for conducting surveys.
- Training of enumerators is crucial to enable them to collect or produce the specialized data from the CV questionnaire.
- Extensive qualitative and quantitative pretesting of the initial CV questionnaire is essential.
- Field protocols for the actual survey should be developed and followed throughout the survey.
- Monitoring of field staff and survey data during the field survey is necessary to ensure the quality of data from the survey.

The initial survey questionnaire described in the previous chapter needs to be finalized through a series of small-scale pretest surveys before conducting a full-blown field survey. The quality and utility of the data and other information from either the pretest or actual survey depend significantly on a well-trained survey team. Thus, training of enumerators and field supervisors is important before any of these surveys are carried out. This chapter begins with a discussion of how to conduct training for field survey staff and then explains how to conduct the pretest and actual field surveys.

Field Enumerator/Coordinator Training[17]

Importance of Training Enumerators

Training enumerators is an integral process of questionnaire design and pretesting. In general, the twofold goal of training enumerators is to (i) help them understand the objectives of the survey and the subject matter contained in the CV scenario; and (ii) provide them with skills needed to conduct high-quality surveys whether it is in-person, self-administered, or using other types of survey mode (i.e., digitized).

While much attention is often placed on the questionnaire design, another critical link in survey implementation is the enumerator. Whittington (2002) noted that poorly trained enumerators often lead to puzzling and

[17] Sections 5.1 and 5.2 draw heavily on Whittington (2002).

inconsistent results as well as enumerator bias.[18] Even the most well-crafted CV scenario may make little sense to respondents if the enumerator fails to communicate the CV information effectively, smoothly, and with sensitivity. On the other hand, enumerators are also instruments for listening to people since they filter messages from the respondents to the CV field supervisor and, hence, can help to minimize distortions.

Thus, training and managing a team of enumerators is not a trivial task, but one that merits the full attention of the CV field supervisor just like designing the CV questionnaire would. Whittington (2002) estimated that on average it takes 4 to 6 weeks to develop a questionnaire, train enumerators, do the pretesting, and revise the questionnaire for final survey implementation. At the end of the process, the expected outputs are a refined questionnaire and a skilled survey team. Nonetheless, he cautioned that this only works best with small surveys or with large surveys in one geographic area.

The quality of data and ultimately the reliability of WTP estimates will depend on the trained enumerators' quality of work. Hence, it is also important to conduct proper recruitment and screening before enumerators are subjected to training and fieldwork. Whittington (2002), noted the pros and cons of choosing university students, government officials, social workers, health professionals, and those from other educational backgrounds as enumerators. While it is important to consider people's backgrounds, profession, and even field experience, character and attitude are what make a good enumerator.[19] The hiring of enumerators is ultimately a judgment call of the CV field supervisor. Whittington (2002) however, advised that an enumerator who is unwilling to follow the CV script and the questionnaire will not be a good interviewer and hence, should not be hired. Box 5.1 discusses some of the common problems encountered in training enumerators and gives guidance on how to address them.

[18] Enumerator bias refers to enumerator-specific results because of an enumerator's willful and/or unconscious deviation from the agreed survey administration protocols.

[19] This includes one's ability to enjoy people and make them feel at ease, be polite and kind in listening to and respecting people's opinion, keep confidential information, be honest and show integrity in reporting the right information as well as being teachable, reliable, flexible, and committed to accomplishing the objectives of the survey.

Box 5.1: Common Difficulties in Training Enumerators

Some common difficulties in training enumerators to conduct CV studies in developing countries are listed below.

1. **Enumerators under-appreciate the importance of each respondent receiving the same CV scenario information.** This leads enumerators to deviate from the script and communicate the CV scenario their own way by adapting it to fit their respondents or a certain situation. Hence, the scenario can change in different ways, which may differ from the original meaning intended by the researcher.

   Response: Use an illustration to show enumerators how sensitive meaning is to changes in the words used. Inform them that they should diligently follow the script to preserve the meaning of the CV scenario and get a consistent and reliable response to the CV question.

2. **Enumerators make efforts to convince respondents that they should be willing to pay for the hypothetical good or service.**

   Response: The CV field supervisor must emphasize to enumerators that the respondents are free to accept a No vote, and it is not their role to change the respondent's mind.

3. **Enumerators do not adjust their behavior and interview style to the personality of the respondent.** This may lead to the respondents' reluctance to answer questions if they do not feel at ease or comfortable with the interviewer during the survey.

   Response: Inform enumerators that they need to be sensitive to and aware of how the respondent is reacting or responding so that they can adjust their behavior accordingly to make the respondent feel comfortable and at ease.

4. **Enumerators use a shortcut and do not obtain high-quality responses to all questions in the CV survey.**

   Response: The importance of avoiding missing entries and "don't know" responses to questions must be stressed during training. Enumerators must be trained to probe for answers and know when a "don't know" response is acceptable. Also, explain clearly to them that under their contract, they will only be paid for interviews with complete and verified entries.

Source: Whittington (2002).

Standard Enumerator Training Practices

To standardize the conduct of CV surveys among enumerators, it is recommended that the CV specialist or CV field supervisor develop a survey protocol and a simple training manual, which field supervisors and enumerators can refer to during the survey implementation. The survey protocol may specify the rules or agreement on the maximum number of questionnaires to be accomplished by each enumerator, methods on survey monitoring, data quality assurance procedures, and other relevant logistic protocols. These simple tools will be helpful especially when multiple teams are simultaneously surveying different sites.

The pitfalls in training enumerators may be minimized during the training process, by giving emphasis on critical areas such as the following:

- **Get enumerator inputs on the draft questionnaire.** The CV specialist or CV field supervisor should review the questionnaire together with the enumerators and get feedback on the questionnaire's overall clarity, flow, and accuracy (especially if a local translation is used). Enumerators are encouraged to ask questions on the technical aspects of the CV scenario to establish a common understanding of the good being valued. The CV scenario must be administered to respondents clearly and consistently.

- **Familiarize enumerators with the survey instrument.** Enumerators must learn how to properly introduce themselves, use logical skip patterns, present visuals, and ask proper and neutral questions. It is important to note that the quality of the survey often improves with time as enumerators become more familiar with the questionnaire.

  Familiarity with the content and the order of questions can increase enumerators' confidence in administering the survey. Being confident allows them to effectively and clearly communicate the content of the survey, thereby making respondents feel more relaxed and comfortable. Familiarity with the questionnaire shortens survey duration, makes respondents more attentive and cooperative, which in turn becomes a guard against respondent fatigue.

- **Ensure that important covariates included in the CV analysis are gathered from the survey.** At the outset, enumerators should be instructed to avoid missing entries for these covariates, especially for bids, household income, and other demographic covariates. The importance of such variables in the analysis needs to be clearly explained to enumerators during training so that they have a better appreciation of the quality of data to be collected.

- **Administer the CV scenario clearly and neutrally using the designed script to minimize potential bias.** This includes important elements such as the baseline and the proposed changes, the payment mechanism, institutional arrangements, reminder of income and budget constraints, entreaties (i.e., cheap talk/oath script), and valuation question with decision rule or provision point mechanisms, among others. Because of the sensitivity of the information provided to respondents in the CV scenario, enumerators must be instructed to closely follow the CV script since it is important for each respondent to be valuing the same good. Any deviation from the script may significantly affect the WTP estimates.

  Thus, enumerators need to be knowledgeable, informed, and familiar with the CV scenario, so that they could correctly respond to those who are likely to ask questions or request for clarification on the elements of the CV scenario. Regular team meetings and feedback can help address these concerns so that response to common questions on the CV scenario can be standardized across enumerators.

- **Create a random sampling of households and random distribution of bids across respondents (if using single dichotomous choice format).** The design and mechanics of random sampling, split sampling, and random bid distribution to respondents should be explained clearly to enumerators as this can negatively affect WTP estimates.

  Explaining the split sample design will avoid confusion among enumerators. A split sample means that different households are given different versions of the questionnaire. Enumerators should be trained to use the questionnaire assigned to a specific household. The same applies to random bid assignments under the dichotomous choice format, which should not be distributed based on the respondents' social class. A common and serious survey error occurs when enumerators assign questionnaires by income class, i.e., households in upper-class subdivisions are given higher bids questionnaires while households in low-cost subdivisions receive lower bids questionnaires.

- **Include the survey protocol in the training manual to guide enumerators.** The training manual should include survey logistics such as the maximum number of questionnaires administered per day to avoid enumerator fatigue and safeguard quality. The enumerator should submit completed questionnaires daily for checking, monitoring, and feedback; report survey nonresponse and use randomly generated replacements; do repeat visits and/or phone callbacks; and participate in team meetings for feedback.

Besides lectures, the enumerators' training must include a variety of learning exercises, such as diagnostic tests, role play with critique,[20] games, and supervised field interviews[21] complemented with debriefing sessions to address problems that may arise during the pretest.

Conducting Survey Pretests

Johnston et al. (2017) noted the lack of pretest guidelines in CV studies even though pretesting is a crucial element in establishing content validity. Two types of pretesting are recommended: (i) qualitative pretesting of the survey instrument using focus groups (FGDs), cognitive interviews, or other small-group methods; and (ii) quantitative pretesting for small samples or pilot studies for a large sample (e.g., Mitchell and Carson 1989; Arrow et al. 1993; Bateman et al. 2002; Champ, Boyle, and Brown 2017). Outputs of qualitative and quantitative pretests should be properly documented.[22]

Qualitative Preparation through a Focus Group Discussion

A focus group discussion (Box 5.2) is considered an efficient method to test scenario descriptions and assess how much and what type of information respondents will need to answer in the valuation questionnaire (Desvousges and Smith 1988; Johnston et al. 1995). As mentioned in the previous chapter, the qualitative pretesting of the questionnaire may also involve verifying or identifying the initial payment or bid range. However, several authors noted that focus groups are prone to group-based effects[23] (Hutchinson and Chilton 1999; Jorgensen 1999; Lunt 1999).

[20] Diagnostic tests are written or oral tests/exams focused on the contents and important nuances of the items in the questionnaire. Role-play games involve mock interviews wherein enumerators and trainers act as respondents for other enumerators.

[21] Mentoring during this stage is done by a trainer who accompanies each enumerator to the field, observes how they do interviews, and provides helpful feedback for improvement. Enumerators should only be used when the trainer is confident that they can do interviews on their own.

[22] This includes FGD scripts or interviews, the number of FGDs conducted, characteristics of participants, subject-selection methods, field test results, key survey-design insights, and resulting design decisions.

[23] Group effect is a type of bias that occurs when participants in a focus group come to a consensus or similar conclusions. Social pressure to conform or the presence of dominant persons in the group may make participants falsely agree with others to reach an answer that is agreed upon by the majority.

Box 5.2: Research Design for the Focus Group Discussion

The focus group discussion (FGD) process begins with the identification of the study's key research objectives. For contingent valuation (CV) studies these include mainly providing feedback and inputs to the critical elements of the CV scenario such as the description of the good (without-project versus with-project), payment vehicle, the institutional mechanism on which the good is to be provided, and the choice of bids. Based on these, the researcher prepares a list of questions that are organized into a script to guide the FGD session. A typical FGD lasts 1–2 hours, usually not longer as participants are likely to suffer from fatigue. The participants including the group composition are identified next. Typically, the decision to adopt a heterogeneous or homogeneous FGD will always depend on the main research goal. Most FGDs in CV studies are conducted with mixed groups except when dealing with sensitive topics (i.e., sanitation and hygiene practices) that may warrant a separate FGD for men and women for self-disclosure to be natural and comfortable. The literature provides evidence of the merits of mixed grouping in terms of the quality of discussion and outcomes (Freitas et al. 1998).

In recruiting FGD participants, the main consideration would be their ability and capacity to provide relevant and useful information. Hence, purposive sampling from the target population is done through the help of local networks and contacts such as local officials or health workers. The CV researcher provides them with the general characteristics of FGD participants to be recruited (i.e., mix composition of age, gender, economic status, etc.). Typically, the ideal FGD size is around 8–12 participants. Since there is no guarantee that all of them will participate, Rabiee (2004) recommends that researchers may over-recruit by 10%–25%. Invitation letters are then sent to preselected participants and follow-ups are done by the local contacts.

Choosing a venue for the FGD must consider the participants' comfort (i.e., adequate space, good lighting, and ventilation), access to the venue, and levels of distraction. The seating arrangement should also enable participants to have an unobstructed view of other participants and the facilitators. Venues may include enclosed spaces in nearby restaurants, halls, or community centers. Also, most FGDs provide "tokens" for participants for their time. Snacks are also provided as well as transportation money for those who need transport to the venue.

It is also critical for the FGD to be handled by a team that will at least include a skilled facilitator and an assistant. If the discussion will be recorded through audio or video, the facilitator must inform the participants and get their consent. The facilitator plays a significant role in the FGD by steering the discussion to

continued on next page

Box 5.2 (continued)

get relevant answers to the key objectives of the study, while creating a relaxed and comfortable environment for participants to openly discuss their views and perceptions. On the other hand, the assistant is tasked with observing and documenting the general content of the discussion including nonverbal interactions and group dynamics.

In regard to how many FGDs must be done, Krueger (1994) put forth the principle of theoretical saturation where FGD sessions are conducted, "until a clear pattern emerges, and subsequent groups produce no new information." In some cases, this can necessitate three to four FGDs, depending on the coverage of the study area and the complexity of the topic.

Source: Authors.

The cognitive interview is another method that can be useful, especially when dealing with sensitive topics and challenging survey design issues is not possible in focus groups. It involves asking respondents individually how they feel about the questions and options in the interview. These methods, however, can be blended in a way that information can be obtained from both the individual and group levels (Powe 2007).

Peer or expert review also provides insights when dealing with technical descriptions in the CV scenario (Groves et al. 2009). Conducting four to six FGDs is recommended, with a larger number of FGDs for new, unfamiliar, or difficult-to-quantify goods.

Pretesting from a Smaller Sample of the Target Population

Another good practice, where feasible, is to undertake quantitative pretesting from a smaller sample of the target population to test the efficacy of bid levels in the valuation question, refine the experimental design, and conduct initial statistical tests of the hypotheses, among others (Johnston et al. 2017).

During pretesting, it is important to obtain the enumerators' feedback on the common questions respondents ask regarding the presentation of the CV scenario. The appropriate response to these questions should be discussed in a group setting where the views of enumerators are taken into consideration before the CV field supervisor proposes a response to their queries (Whittington 2002).

The sample size for the pretest would depend on the number of CV scenarios (split sample) and bid price levels. Typically, a minimum of 30 samples is recommended per bid for the initial analysis, and more than one round of pilot survey is usually needed.

Conducting extensive pretests provides several benefits to the CV field supervisor such as (i) serving as a training avenue for enumerators; (ii) helping to determine the suitability of the commodity/service definition; (iii) gauging the appropriateness of the bid range for a credible WTP result; (iv) facilitating the precoding of open-ended responses for data entry and analysis; (v) assisting in identifying common mistakes by observing how enumerators conduct the survey; (vi) finalizing survey logistics; and (vii) giving the researcher some degree of confidence that the questionnaire is appropriate and ready for use.

Assessing the bid range and distribution during pretesting is imperative. The desired result is that 90% of the respondents should be accepting (or choosing, in the case of a payment card elicitation format) at least the lowest bid. On the other hand, only 10% of the respondents should be voting or choosing the highest bid. If this bid distribution is not observed then the minimum and maximum bids should be recalibrated through another round of pretesting. Sometimes several pretest iterations are required before this desired bid range is achieved.

Conducting Field Interviews

The main concern in conducting CV surveys is to safeguard the quality of the field data and minimize nonresponse among survey respondents. Whittington (2002) cites poor administration and execution of surveys among the reasons why contingent valuation in developing countries is at times problematic. Attention to survey execution can help better ensure reliable estimates.

Questionnaire Submission

The survey administrator should set a quota for completed questionnaires per day to ensure data quality and guard against "interviewer fatigue." Depending on the length of the CV survey instrument (see Box 5.3), the prescribed quota could range from four to six questionnaires per day per enumerator. Enumerators are instructed to keep to this protocol unless there are valid reasons for doing more than the prescribed quota.

Box 5.3: Duration of a CV Survey

CV surveys for project economic analysis are often conducted as part of broader socioeconomic and poverty assessment surveys. The advantage of this practice is that it brings time and budget savings, and practicality in terms of survey administration. However, this practice entails a longer interview time, a greater cognitive burden on respondents, and a high risk of respondent fatigue, which may ultimately compromise valuation results. More importantly, it also means that the sample is unlikely to be representative of the beneficiary population. Implementing a stand-alone CV survey whenever possible is likely to maximize attention and minimize enumeration and analytical challenges.

As much as possible, the average interview time should be kept at 45 minutes[a] to minimize respondent fatigue. Hence, the questionnaire must be carefully designed to include only questions that are relevant to the study. Adhering to the rules of good interview practices (see Appendix 6) can also shorten the time spent in doing interviews. Interview length should be a factor that is anticipated during the questionnaire development stage.

[a] Beyond this, the enumerator must ask for the respondents' permission to continue with the interview or to return another time if the respondent says no.
Source: Authors.

After completing the daily quota, enumerators are instructed to "clean" the questionnaires before submission. Cleaning the questionnaire does not mean changing the respondent's answer, filling out blank items, or making personal interpretations of comments made by the respondents. Rather, "cleaning" pertains to the need to finalize entries[24] by writing answers—including comments and final computations—legibly in the designated spaces of the survey form. It may also entail translating comments from the local language into English.

Completing the Questionnaire

Survey teams usually employ a strict policy for accepting questionnaires. Questionnaires with missing, inconsistent, and doubtful entries must be completed through callbacks, which includes a return visit to the respondent's home or a follow-up phone call. Use of computer-assisted personal interview (CAPI) software for survey administration on tablet or laptop computers can help to include checks to assure data quality, facilitate

[24] Typically for manual surveys, enumerators are encouraged to use a pencil in filling out the questionnaire during the survey, hence, some marks may not be clear and legible. During "cleaning" they are instructed to use a pen so that the encoder can easily read the answers.

real time data submission for further checks, and enable enumerators to be closely monitored.

Survey Logistics

The overall goal for survey logistics is to be able to properly administer the final survey to the predetermined sample in each time frame. Overseeing the survey implementation is the task of the CV specialist, the CV field supervisors, and the local field coordinators.[25]

When SBDC or DBDC methods are used, the survey forms need to be unique for each respondent and must reflect a randomized bid amount. This means that survey forms need to be printed according to the randomization with the bid and respondent identifiers, and that extra forms need to be preprinted for replacements if the survey is conducted on paper. CAPI methods can embed the randomization in the survey software.

Size of the survey team

The size of the survey team usually depends on the survey time frame, sample size/number of respondents, sampling strategy, and the available budget. Usually the CV field supervisor (or the CV specialist) makes the main decisions during the field survey. A local field coordinator can assist, particularly in the logistics and in assuring the quality of survey outputs. The number of field coordinators will also depend on the size of the project survey scope or sampling frame. The advantage of including field coordinators is to ensure that all survey forms are completed, checked, and verified before they are sent to the survey firm for encoding or data analysis (in the case of digitized surveys). The number of enumerators will also depend on the total number of surveys and the survey schedule. For a small coverage, four or five enumerators may be reasonable, but more are likely to be required for a larger coverage. The role of each survey team member should be clearly explained during the training and defined in their contract, which should include grounds for its revocation.

Monitoring survey progress

To monitor the progress of the survey, each enumerator should submit to the field coordinator or the CV field supervisor their monitoring form daily,

[25] The local field coordinator can also be the most senior and experienced enumerator.

which should include the randomly generated names from the sample (if one is available) as well as the name of any replacements. Enumerators should also note the respondent's reasons for refusing to be interviewed. The survey team should have a "field operation center" where team meetings are held and where questionnaires are distributed to and submitted by enumerators for checking and verification. As much as possible, submitted questionnaires that need verification or completion should be followed up with immediate callbacks.

Risks and safety of the survey team

The CV field supervisor or field coordinator should be cognizant of any potential risks enumerators may face during the survey. This includes conducting interviews after dark or in unsafe neighborhoods. To lessen the risk, enumerators may do the interview in pairs or have someone from the locality or village, such as local health workers or officials, accompany them.[26] If they are conducting interviews in various locations across the locality, a vehicle may be arranged to drop them off and pick them up at a designated time and place.

Incentives for survey enumerators

To motivate enumerators to perform well, three types of compensation can be given: money, references, and connections for future work (Whittington 2002). Monetary compensation can be a rate per day or per questionnaire, depending on the norm in the local area. From experience, payment per approved questionnaire with a daily quota (such as a maximum of six questionnaires per day) is an adequate incentive, if the rate is fair or commensurate with the time and effort spent in doing high-quality interviews. The rate should also be high enough to encourage them to perform well and should be based on prevailing wage rates in the local area for the relevant education/skill level of similar workers—for example, offering them twice the minimum rate as an incentive.

Meanwhile, a nonmonetary incentive includes providing enumerators with formal certificates that acknowledge their work and contribution to the project. Whittington (2002) includes the names, addresses, and contact numbers of their enumerators in the appendix of the report so that they can be contacted by future researchers. Also, it is equally important to create

[26] In the Philippines, barangay health workers and officials often serve as "guides" to enumerators and are given a daily allowance for the extra help they provide in ensuring enumerators are safe and secure.

an atmosphere of fun, learning, and ownership among the members of the survey team to keep them motivated and focused on the goal.

Field Supervision

Good field supervision completes the process of guaranteeing the quality of data gathered from the field. Fieldwork quality can only be assured when a clear and systematic supervision procedure such as the one described below is in place.

1. **Daily review and check completed questionnaires for feedback.** Though time-consuming, this practice benefits the survey by setting a standard of quality for enumerators to adhere to; allows common mistakes to be promptly identified and corrected such as inconsistent/missing entries; creates opportunities for field supervisors to get to know the enumerators; permits supervisors to form a standard interpretation of responses to certain questions; and prepares the questionnaire for data entry. Although this practice may not be feasible in national surveys, it should be done as much as possible in CV studies.
2. **Establish a system of spot checks, back checks, and high frequency checks.** Spot checks are random instances of observations by supervisors on enumerator performance in the field using a set protocol. Back checks are random reinterviews of respondents by supervisors or other enumerators besides those who conducted the main interview. High frequency checks are automated processes of checking to ensure that collected data are within plausible ranges, are internally consistent, and are complete, which are conducted in real time for CAPI surveys. CAPI surveys also generate metadata that can be useful to track enumerator actions in the field and ensure fidelity of survey conduct.
3. **Assess the quality of the enumerator's performance.** It is also important for enumerators to receive feedback on areas that need improvement. The field supervisor does this by accompanying them and observing how they handle actual interviews, i.e., administering the CV scenario. Mentoring is purposively done during the first week of the survey until the field supervisor has a certain degree of confidence that the enumerator can do it on their own with minimal supervision.
4. **Ensure that enumerators interview the intended sample and replacements that were randomly drawn from the sampling frame.** Random checks are very helpful in spotting cases of falsified questionnaires or when enumerators have not followed the sampling

frame. This is done by randomly selecting respondents from the completed survey forms and visiting them soon after the interview to verify if they were indeed interviewed and if the questionnaire entries match their answers. Hence, a complete and detailed address of the respondent is needed. The enumerators may accompany the field supervisor during random checks, or they may seek help from local officials or health workers who are familiar with the respondents' addresses.

In addition to these components, part of the field supervision protocol is to terminate poorly performing and dishonest enumerators. At the outset, enumerators must be informed of this contract clause, which is tied to their work performance and in turn their continued employment.[27] Grounds for dismissal may include falsifying survey data, revealing confidential information, or refusing to follow survey protocols. This process ensures that everyone understands the high standard of quality required in CV surveys. The use of CAPI, on the other hand, can facilitate and automate survey monitoring. Real time uploading of survey data to the "cloud" permits instantaneous and remote checking of data validity and enumerator progress.

Ethical Considerations in CV Surveys

CV surveys can mislead or confuse the respondent and spread confusion to the study population in three main ways (Whittington 2004):

1. **Providing background information in the contingent valuation scenario.** Wrong information on the hypothetical program or policy may harm respondents. An example provided by Whittington (2004) is using a prevalence rate of HIV/AIDS in the CV scenario that is less than the actual figure in the city where the respondent lives. This may prompt the respondent to discontinue precautionary measures currently undertaken and, hence, may likely increase the risk of contracting the virus. Thus, the CV field supervisor should check the accuracy of the technical information used in framing the CV scenario.
2. **Describing the hypothetical market or choice problem.** Some respondents may misinterpret the hypothetical scenario in the CV survey to be real. This may be due to the limitation of the local

[27] While actions need to be done swiftly and decisively, they must also be done in a deliberate manner with the survey team. The rest of the enumerators can help the CV supervisor or specialist decide how best to handle the situation if it arises (Whittington 2002).

dialect in translating a counterfactual condition such as the choice being “only hypothetical” or respondents being told to “suppose” or “imagine” a scenario being described, which may not actually or necessarily be offered (Whittington 1996). These nuances are often lost in translation. Hence, as much as possible, the CV field supervisor can include in the translated CV script the keywords enumerators would need to emphasize when explaining the CV scenario to the respondents.

3. **Using split sample experimental design.** The experimental design in CV surveys often uses a split sample to estimate the respondents’ WTP and test the reliability and consistency of these estimates across different subsamples. The problem arises when respondents talk to each other (which is possible in a close-knit rural community) and discover that they were given different bids or different versions of the questionnaire. This creates confusion and in certain instances negative reactions over the thought of being “fooled” by the enumerators. To avoid such incidents, the enumerator can inform respondents that they are given different prices (bids) or questionnaire versions as part of the study design, to determine how they would respond to a hypothetical situation in which they are asked to make a real economic commitment for a good or service.

4. **Providing compensation.** Another ethical concern in conducting CV surveys is that of compensating respondents. In developing countries, it is generally not recommended to provide monetary compensation to respondents, as doing so may influence their answer and create precedence for similar work in the future. However, some surveys provide a small token of appreciation to respondents who agreed to be interviewed, especially if the duration of the survey takes longer than 45 minutes. Preferably, this should not be in monetary terms.

CHAPTER 6
MANAGING AND ANALYZING CVM DATA

```
. xi: logit accept bid age gender knowledge i.incomecat
i.incomecat       _Iincomecat_1-5     (naturally coded; _Iincomecat_1 omitted)

Iteration 0:   log likelihood = -1716.9293
Iteration 1:   log likelihood = -1069.7412
Iteration 2:   log likelihood = -1062.7898
Iteration 3:   log likelihood = -1062.7643
Iteration 4:   log likelihood = -1062.7643

Logistic regression                             Number of obs     =      2,500
                                                LR chi2(8)        =    1308.33
                                                Prob > chi2       =     0.0000
Log likelihood = -1062.7643                     Pseudo R2         =     0.3810

------------------------------------------------------------------------------
      accept |      Coef.   Std. Err.      z    P>|z|     [95% Conf. Interval]
-------------+----------------------------------------------------------------
         bid |  -.0275436   .0010303   -26.73   0.000    -.0295629   -.0255243
         age |   .0453171    .014149     3.20   0.001     .0175855    .0730486
      gender |   .4730452    .188012     2.52   0.012     .1045484     .841542
   knowledge |   .0407688   .0434707     0.94   0.348    -.0444323    .1259699
_Iincomecat_2 |    .195424   .2217065     0.88   0.378    -.2391129    .6299608
_Iincomecat_3 |   .5580804   .2018386     2.76   0.006      .162484    .9536769
_Iincomecat_4 |   .6173363   .2018349     3.06   0.002     .2217472    1.012925
```

Key Messages:

- Regressions are important tools for quantitative analysis of CVM data.
- Descriptive analysis of CVM data should at the minimum include (i) discussion of the bid distribution, and (ii) cross-tabulations between WTP and important variables.
- The appropriate regression model depends on the elicitation format and the nature of the dependent variable it produces.
- It is important to check and report the convergent, construct, and content validity of the WTP estimates.

Once the field survey is done, the raw data are processed, encoded, cleaned, and prepared for analysis. The initial analysis of processed data usually involves a qualitative discussion of data patterns and a quantitative discussion which is typically facilitated by regression analysis. This chapter discusses good practices in managing CV data and describes the current regression models that are used in analyzing processed CV data.

Data Management

In the context of a CV study, the primary goal of data management is to produce high-quality understandable data that are usable not only for the subsequent willingness-to-pay (WTP) analysis, but also for other researchers who may want to use them for other studies or replicate the results of the study. Data management is an iterative process that largely starts in the field. Irregularities such as ID duplication and inconsistent and missing variable entries should be identified and resolved in the field through consultation and constant communication between the field staff and the project proponents.

Encoding

If a pen-and-paper personal interview (PAPI) protocol is used during the survey, data from the field are encoded manually, and this is best done with a database program such as CSPro or Microsoft Access, to name a few. Although an Excel spreadsheet could also be used, the limitations discourage its use. First, data consistency checks cannot be programmed in Excel, hence, making the encoding process prone to error. Second, Excel cannot store data variables and labels. Double entry, or having two different encoders encoding separately is a practice that can help to avoid encoding errors.

Using a computer-aided personal interview (CAPI) can save time in implementing a CV study because it bypasses the encoding stage and allows consistency checks (provided these are incorporated into the electronic questionnaire). Data stored in the server or cloud can easily be downloaded along with the variables and data labels, if available. It also allows real time monitoring of data as they are completed from the field survey. CAPI-based surveys, however, require a more extensive questionnaire pretesting than PAPI-based interviews.

Once data are downloaded or encoded, the original file should be preserved in a raw format. Changes and corrections in the data should be saved in a different file to easily revert to the original data in case of errors in the data cleaning process. A codebook for this raw file should also be created so that users, project team members, or outsiders could familiarize themselves with the details of the original data. Changes in the raw file should be documented to allow efficient tracing when problems or doubts arise about how data were processed. This process also promotes transparency on how the final data set was produced. In Stata, do-files with generous use of instructions, notes, and annotations make the entire data cleaning process not only easy to follow but also transparent and open to scrutiny and correction.

Data Cleaning

The World Bank's Development Impact Evaluation has developed a checklist that may help simplify this task (Box 6.1). The checklist highlights some essential data-cleaning needs such as the following:

a) Checking for the uniqueness of the respondent's ID
b) Recoding and checking the validity of missing values
c) Labeling of variables and values (if PAPI protocol is used)
d) Renaming of variables
e) Standardization of units and checking the conversion of physical units
f) Checking for outliers
g) Checking for variable inconsistencies

Box 6.1: Data Cleaning Checklist

1.0	**Before data cleaning: Importing the data**
1.1	Check for importing issues such as broken lines when importing .csv files
1.2	Make sure you have unique IDs
1.3	De-identify all data and save in a new .dta file
1.4	Never make any changes to the raw data
2.0	**Important steps for data cleaning**
2.1	Label variables, don't use special characters
2.2	Recode and label missing values: your data set should not have observations with -777, -88, or -9 values, for example
2.3	Encode variables: all categorical variables should be saved as labeled numeric variables, no strings
2.4	Don't change variable names from the questionnaire, except for nested, repeat groups, and reshaped roster data
2.5	Check sample representativeness of age, gender, urban/rural, region, and religion
2.6	Check administrative data such as date, time, interviewer variables included
2.7	Test variables consistency
2.8	Identify and document outliers
2.9	Compress data set so it is saved in the most efficient format
2.10	Save cleaned data set with an informative name. Avoid saving in a very recent Stata version
3.0	**Optional steps in data cleaning**
3.1	Order variables – unique ID always first, then same order as questionnaire
3.2	Drop variables that only make sense for questionnaire review (duration, notes, calculations)
3.3	Rename roster variables
3.4	Categorize variables listed as "others"
3.5	Add metadata as notes: original survey question, relevance, constraints, etc.

Source: The World Bank. Development Impact Evaluation. Checklist: Data Cleaning. https://dimewiki.worldbank.org/wiki/Checklist:_Data_Cleaning.

De-Identification

After several checks, data should be de-identified—which means removing the names of respondents and other information that can identify them—before they are stored in the final clean data file. De-identification is part of the confidentiality clause or agreement between the CV study proponent and the respondent. The final clean data should be stored separately in a different file from the raw file. A codebook should also be produced for this final data set.

Qualitative Analysis of CV Data

Once the data set is ready, qualitative analysis can be performed. Qualitative analysis is usually an in-depth description of patterns in the data that can be used to explain the results of the quantitative analysis or regression. The types of qualitative data analysis in the succeeding discussions comprise only the minimum that should be presented. Other discussions should be guided by the research question the project proponents seek to answer. One potential issue to bear in mind before analyzing the data is that unforeseen circumstances in the field may lead to a less-than-ideal representativeness of the sample. Nonresponse and discarded questionnaires due to poor respondent answers are among the main causes of a final survey sample that is unrepresentative of the population of interest. In this case, weights may be used when analyzing and describing the clean survey data (see Box 6.2 on how to derive corrective weights for nonrepresentative data).

Descriptive Summary Statistics

At the minimum, the researcher should compute descriptive statistics (e.g., mean and standard deviations) for the basic characteristics or features of the data set. These statistics show the central tendencies of important variables, the dispersion around the central measure, and the number of observations for each variable. They also serve as a data check since they can be used to locate outliers and missing values. The dispersion of data for a variable often influences the inference or hypothesis testing involving the variable.

Box 6.2: Correcting for Nonrepresentative Samples

Ideally, every element in the population must have an equal probability of being sampled. However, field conditions may be far from ideal. Nonresponse, inaccurate sampling frames, and bad survey responses are some of the non-ideal conditions that may lead to an unrepresentative final survey sample. In such instances, observations should be weighted so that sample statistics will represent that of the population. These weights should be inversely proportional to the probability of being selected. This means that weights of greater than 1 are given to undersampled observations or groups and weights of less than 1 to oversampled groups.

For example, suppose the population is equal to 100 and group A has a population of 70 while group B has a population of 30. Thus, there is a 70% and 30% probability of being included for groups A and B, respectively. Suppose a sample of 60 respondents was determined and 30 respondents were obtained for both groups A and B, the sample probability is therefore 50% for each group. Clearly, group A is undersampled while group B is oversampled. The appropriate sampling weights to correct for the unrepresentativeness of the sample would be 1.40 for group A (i.e., 70/50) and 0.60 (i.e., 30/50) for group B.

In one of the ADB projects reviewed by the study team, the survey sampling design covered a disproportionately larger number of lower-income and vulnerable households within the project site. Upon casual inspection of the income distribution from the population, it showed that the sampled household revealed a nonrepresentativeness of the sample. Thus, to calculate and adjust the WTP value, weights were used to correct for the income bias—the weights used were the ratios of the population and sample distribution in each income category.

Source: Authors.

Cross-Tabulations and Correlation Analysis

Cross-tabulations and correlation analysis will help understand and interpret the answers to the primary valuation question. They also lend credibility to the responses and can lead to adjustments that enhance the reliability of the results (Arrow et al. 1993). The yes or no vote in the single-bounded dichotomous choice (SBDC) analysis should be cross tabulated with the respondent's income and behavioral and knowledge variables. Correlation analysis between the bid levels and relevant variables can be done for continuous bid data, such as those used in payment card elicitation formats.

Bid Distribution

Another essential type of qualitative analysis is the visualization of the bid distribution, which is usually presented in a histogram that shows the percentage of yes votes per bid in a single-bounded dichotomous CV study. Ideally, the histogram should show a rule of thumb indicating a 90% yes vote on the lowest bid and a 10% yes vote on the highest bid; thus, giving the assurance that the CV study has captured the full range of values for the good or service improvement.

Subgroup Data Analysis

Aside from analyzing data for the whole sample, the qualitative analysis can also be done for sample subgroups. Disaggregation of data should reflect at the very least, the stratified or cluster sampling that is part of the survey strategy. For example, descriptive statistics can be compared across small political units or villages if stratification or clustering was done using this grouping. Likewise, bid distribution can be presented for both the whole sample and the constructed strata. This subgroup analysis can reveal the difference in preferences and WTP between subgroups.

Quantitative Analysis of CV Data

Regression analysis is the primary quantitative analysis used for a CV study. It gives useful information pertaining to the factors affecting respondent decisions. The information produced by regression results can also be used to identify policies that can enhance or increase support for the program or project as well as aid in policy targeting. Furthermore, regression results help assess the validity of the CV study and check whether the results conform to standard economic theory. Finally, the WTP estimate is also derived from the regression results.

The type of data used as the dependent variable in the regression model depends on the elicitation format. Thus, selecting the appropriate regression model for the analysis is likewise determined by the design of the questionnaire and the chosen elicitation format. The single-bounded dichotomous choice format produces a binary dependent variable, hence, the logit or probit regression models would be appropriate for this format.

Payment card bid formats, on the other hand, produce data intervals as dependent variables. If a point estimate—either the midpoint or lower bound of the interval—is used as the dependent variable then some form of censoring would occur, making the Tobit regression model more appropriate in this case. When the intervals themselves are used as the dependent variable, the more appropriate models would be the interval regression or the ordered probit. The next sections show how these regression models are implemented and how regression results are used to calculate WTP estimates. Appendix 7 discusses the appropriate econometric models for the different elicitation formats used in a CV study.

Preparing the Data from an SBDC Elicitation Format

To prepare the data for regression, the dependent variable should be constructed as a binary variable with a value equal to 1 if the respondent signifies acceptance of the price/bid (also referred to as a "yes" vote for the referendum), and 0 otherwise. This binary dependent variable can be regressed against a variety of independent variables or regressors. The selection of variables as regressors varies depending on the problem at hand. The choice of regressors represents what is believed to be the data-generating process and is always guided by economic theory—at the very least, must include a price (bid value) and an income variable (Box 6.3 discusses the issues in defining income). Both variables are treated as exogenous, or fully independent.

Other important variables whose omission in the model could lead to inconsistent estimates are as follows.

a) **Sociodemographic variables.** These give characteristics of the household head, such as age, gender, primary occupation, and education level.

b) **Behavioral variables.** These variables vary across the context of the problem. For example, if the good being valued pertains to changes in water quality through an investment in forest conservation, variables such as respondent's participation in environment- or conservation-related activities can be included.

c) **Knowledge and attitudinal variables.** These variables gauge the respondent's knowledge of the intervention and its effects. In the previous example, this could be knowledge regarding forest conservation and its relationship with hydrologic functions or opinions regarding issues related to forest conservation.

Variables should be selected with care, especially behavioral variables, as most of them can introduce some level of endogeneity in the regression model. Endogeneity, which refers to explanatory variables that are actually determined in part by the dependent variable, leads to inconsistent estimates—which is crucial since, as shown in Appendix 7, parameter estimates are used to derive the WTP estimate. For instance, if the good being valued is an improvement in water quality and the behavioral variable included in the regression is the household decision to boil water, this variable will most likely be correlated with the household's preference for clean water, which is part of the error term.

The respondent's knowledge level is usually measured through a series of questions and indicators. The results of the focus group discussion as well as feedback and observations of field survey staff can guide the selection of the appropriate variables to represent knowledge of the good and related issues. Another way to identify the relevant knowledge variables is to select them based on statistical procedures such as the principal component analysis (PCA), which allows the identification and removal of redundant data from multiple and related questions.

Box 6.3: Issues and Options in Designing Questions on Income

The willingness to pay for a particular product or service is the maximum amount of money an individual or household is willing to pay depending on several factors, one of which is income. Since income is an important influence on willingness to pay, the survey instrument must include the necessary questions that will capture this information as accurately as possible. However, there are two principal challenges in collecting and measuring income data: (i) given the many potential sources of income, asking multiple questions can be quite a burden to respondents; and (ii) income is a sensitive topic, and respondents may find questions about income in surveys intrusive (Davern et al. 2005).

The following information can be used as a guide when designing questions about income for a contingent valuation survey:

- Unit: household or individual's personal income
- Definition: gross, net, or disposable income
- Measurement: one single summary question on income or collect detailed information on different income components
- Reference period: monthly or yearly income
- Response categories: exact income amounts or predefined income bands

continued on next page

Box 6.3 (continued)

Household or individual income: The consideration of whether to collect household or personal income should depend on the specific research interest and objective (Khun 2019). Household income is a better measure for living standard or socioeconomic status than personal income, assuming that financial resources are shared between household members. For specific research questions, such as those seeking to look at the influence of income on specific opinions or decisions, personal income may be more appropriate than household income. In CVM, household income may be more appropriate for studies that involve household decision-making or projects that affect the general household (such as piped water supply or centralized heating), while personal income may be more than adequate measure for projects that involve personal decisions (such as use of improved public spaces or access to rehabilitated tourist or heritage sites).

Gross, net, or disposable income: Many surveys collect data with just a single question without qualifying whether what is being measured is gross (before taxes and other deductions such as social security contributions, and cost of health-care premiums), net (after taxes and deductions), or disposable income. For many research and data analyses, disposable income would be an adequate measure for analysis as it reflects living standards, available resources, and socioeconomic status more accurately. In addition, these three income concepts vary in definition in many countries, which must be taken into consideration when designing the questionnaire.

Single or multiple questions: The use of a single question is designed in part to reduce the respondent's burden and increase response rate but may lead to loss in accuracy and information. Multiple question formats give a breakdown of an individual's or household's income sources, offering greater accuracy and flexibility in income calculation but at a greater survey cost. For multiple questions on income, one can include these various types of income sources: salary/employment income, self-employment and business income, social security and pensions, welfare or disability allowance, court-ordered alimony and child support, gained interest and income from investments, and rental income.

Reference period: Another important point to consider in designing the income question in surveys is the reference period, i.e., whether to ask for monthly or yearly income. While annual income is the international standard for income measures, Boheim and Jenkins (2006) found that it introduces an increased risk of recall bias and erroneous calculation. Asking for monthly income may have several advantages such as ease of recall especially for

continued on next page

Box 6.3 (continued)

salary and employment income, or social security/pension payments. Monthly income data can also be calculated to generate annual income with additional information on the number of months during which the income is received.

Response categories: Recording income can be done in different ways such as by asking open-ended questions or an exact amount of income, or by selecting an income band from a list of options. The use of income bands tend to improve response quality but introduces a loss of information on the within-band variation, whereas collection of income without bands requires data cleaning and decisions on how to treat outliers after data collection. In CVM applications, income bands or ranges are preferred as they have been seen to reduce nonresponse compared with open-ended questions.

Source: Khun (2019); Authors.

Estimation from an SBDC Elicitation Format

A logistic regression of the form below is used to estimate the relationship between bid acceptance, bid amount, and respondent characteristics.

$$Pr(yes)=Pr\left(\left(\beta_0+\sum^{K}\beta_k X_k+\sum^{I}\beta_{Yi}Y_i-\gamma_{1Y}b+\varepsilon\right)>0\right)$$

Where X_k is a vector of variables that affect the utility of the individual, Y_i is the income level of the individual, β_k, β_{Yi} are their coefficients, β_0 is the intercept, $\gamma_{1Y}b$ is the coefficient of the bid variable, and ε is the error term.

The theoretical and empirical foundation of the SBDC regression is discussed in more detail in Appendix 7. This subsection discusses the practical analysis of SBDC data using Stata.[28] The logit regression model is more commonly used in analyzing SBDC data because of the ease of working with its functional form. Its difference from the probit regression model, which is based on a normal distribution, is relatively minor. A logit regression is run in Stata using the logit command. Figure 6.1 gives an example of a Stata output for this command. The analysis in this and the following sections are based on a synthetic data set generated by the authors for the regression walk-throughs.

[28] For analyzing CVM data using R, an excellent reference is Aizaki, Nakatani, and Sato (2015).

Figure 6.1: Logit Regression Command and Output in Stata

```
. xi: logit accept bid age gender knowledge i.incomecat
i.incomecat       _Iincomecat_1-5     (naturally coded; _Iincomecat_1
omitted)

Iteration 0:   log likelihood = -1716.9293
Iteration 1:   log likelihood = -1069.7412
Iteration 2:   log likelihood = -1062.7898
Iteration 3:   log likelihood = -1062.7643
Iteration 4:   log likelihood = -1062.7643

Logistic regression                             Number of obs     =      2,500
                                                LR chi2(8)        =    1308.33
                                                Prob > chi2       =     0.0000
Log likelihood = -1062.7643                     Pseudo R2         =     0.3810

------------------------------------------------------------------------------
      accept | Coef.       Std. Err.      z     P>|z|   [95% Conf. Interval]
-------------+----------------------------------------------------------------
bid          | -.0275436   .0010303   -26.73   0.000   -.0295629   -.0255243
age          |  .0453171    .014149     3.20   0.001    .0175855    .0730486
gender       |  .4730452    .188012     2.52   0.012    .1045484     .841542
knowledge    |  .0407688   .0434707     0.94   0.348   -.0444323    .1259699
_Iincomecat_2 |   .195424   .2217065     0.88   0.378   -.2391129    .6299608
_Iincomecat_3 |  .5580804   .2018386     2.76   0.006     .162484    .9536769
_Iincomecat_4 |  .6173363   .2018349     3.06   0.002    .2217472    1.012925
_Iincomecat_5 |  .3057421    .201195     1.52   0.129   -.0885929     .700077
cons         |  2.170303      .5295     4.10   0.000    1.132502    3.208104
------------------------------------------------------------------------------
```

Source: Authors.

In Figure 6.1, the dependent variable is labeled as the accept variable, which as discussed earlier is a binary variable (i.e., assumes a 1 or 0 value). Note also that the income variable, which is originally constructed as a continuous variable, is conveniently expanded to a set of categorical or dummy variables using the *xi* command in Stata. That is, income was converted to response categories (see discussion on various ways of collecting and measuring income in Box 6.3).

Presenting and Interpreting the SBDC Regression Results

At a minimum, regression results that are to be presented and interpreted should include the following: (i) coefficient estimates; (ii) standard error of each estimate; (iii) the significance level of each coefficient estimate; (iv) the final number of samples used in the regression; and (v) the indicators of model significance. Figure 6.2 illustrates how regression outputs should be reported.

Figure 6.2: Sample of Reporting Regression Results from SBDC Data

Results of Logit Regression

Dependent Variable	Accept
Independent Variables	Coefficient
Constant/Intercept	2.170*** (0.530)[a]
Bid	-0.028*** (0.001)
Age	0.045*** (0.014)
Gender (Male =1; Female=0)	0.473** (0.190)
Knowledge	0.041 (0.043)
Income Categories:	
Income Category 2	0.195 (0.222)
Income Category 3	0.558*** (0.202)
Income Category 4	0.617*** (0.202)
Income Category 5	0.306 (0.201)
Log-likelihood	-1602.764
Chi squared (8)	1308.330
N	2500

*** = significant at 1%; ** = significant at 5%; * = significant at 10%.
[a] Standard errors in parentheses.
Source: Authors' estimates.

To evaluate the parameters of the estimated model, a test of significance of individual coefficients or parameters is customary. Unlike in ordinary least squares, coefficient values from a probit or logit regression are not the marginal effects of each variable. The discussion of the regression results should therefore concentrate on interpreting the significance and signs of the coefficients. A significant and positive estimated coefficient of a variable is therefore interpreted as being associated with increasing the likelihood of agreeing to an offered bid. It can also be interpreted as a variable that is associated with increasing the likelihood of supporting a program or voting yes for it.

It is wrong to interpret the sign of variable coefficients as affecting the respondent's willingness to pay. For example, in Figure 6.2, the positive coefficient of the income variable may be interpreted as "increases in income are associated with increases in the respondent's WTP." This is an incorrect interpretation. The sign of the coefficient indicates the direction of the relationship between the variable and the dependent variable, which is the likelihood of a yes vote and not the WTP per se. WTP is the amount of income, which when taken from the respondent, will leave them indifferent to the project and pre-project utility and is the measure of value that must be calculated after the regression. This conceptual distinction between estimated coefficients and overall WTP is often overlooked.

The sign of the coefficients of the bid and income variables is important in testing the validity of the CV study. To be consistent with economic theory, the coefficient of the income variable should be positive and significant. In contrast, the coefficient of the offered price/bid should be negative and significant. If the signs of these coefficients are not as expected, doubt is cast on the results of the CV study which then requires a reanalysis of the data.

Finally, the goodness-of-fit measure should also be reported. The first goodness-of-fit measures the log of the likelihood ratio.[29] The other possible goodness-of-fit measure would be to use the fitted probabilities for each respondent. Once this is calculated, an arbitrary cutoff of 50% may be used. Fitted probabilities that are greater than 50% are converted to 1 and otherwise, to zero. This is cross tabulated with the actual 1–0 values for each respondent, which will indicate whether the yes (or 1) is over- or underpredicted by the estimated regression model.

Deriving the WTP Estimates from SBDC Data

The basic formula for WTP is given below (and explained in Appendix 7 in further detail).

$$E[WTP|\beta_0,\beta_k,\gamma_{1Y}] = \frac{\widehat{\beta_0} + \sum_K \widehat{\beta_k} X_k + \sum_l \widehat{\beta_{Y_i}} Yi}{\widehat{\gamma_{1Y}}}$$

[29] This is just 2*log(full model likelihood – intercept only likelihood) which is distributed as chi-squared.

Where, γ_0 is the intercept, $\widehat{\beta_0}$, $\widehat{\beta_k}$,$\widehat{\beta_{Yi}}$ are the estimated parameters from the regressions, and $\widehat{\gamma_{1Y}}$ is the estimated coefficient of the bid variable.

There are three ways of implementing this in Stata. The first approach is to use the sample means of the independent variables and multiply these means with the estimated coefficients from the logit/probit regression and then divide these by the estimated coefficient of the bid variable.

When performing this step, it is important to consider whether the sample is representative of the beneficiary population. If it is not, beneficiary means should be substituted for sample means in the process. The same consideration applies to all methods described here.

After generating the sample means of the independent variables, the *nlcom* command of Stata can be used to compute for the WTP. The *nlcom* computes nonlinear combinations of parameters estimated after a regression or estimation. Figure 6.3 shows how the *nlcom* is set up to produce the WTP estimate, WTP2.

Figure 6.3: Using Sample Means to Compute for WTP after a Logit Regression

```
. nlcom (WTP2: -1*(_b[_cons]+_b[_Iincomecat_2]*_Iincomecat_2_m
+_b[_Iincomecat_3]*_Iincomecat_3_m+_b
> [_Iincomecat_4]*_Iincomecat_4_m+_b[_Iincomecat_5]*_Iincomecat_5_
m+ _b[age]*age_m + _b[gender]*gend
> er_m + _b[knowledge]*knowledge_m)/_b[bid]), noheader

-------------------------------------------------------------
accept |    Coef.    Std. Err.     z     P>|z|    [95% Conf.
                                                  Interval]
-------------+-----------------------------------------------
WTP2   |  164.9238   1.978232   83.37   0.000    161.0465  168.801
-------------------------------------------------------------
```

Source: Authors.

In Figure 6.3, the _b[*variable name*] is used to access the parameter estimates stored in Stata's memory. These stored parameters are multiplied by their corresponding sample means generated earlier. The final output of *nlcom* is the mean WTP and its 95% confidence interval.

The second approach to implementing the mean WTP formula for SBDC data is to generate a WTP for each respondent and take the sample mean of the respondent-specific WTPs. Figure 6.4 shows how this is coded in Stata. The predicted value of the model is generated after the logit regression, as shown in Figure 6.4. This is the numerator of the mean WTP formula discussed in Appendix 7. However, the predicted value includes the value of the product of the offered bid and its estimated coefficient. This value needs to be subtracted from the predicted value, to be consistent with the mean WTP formula. The second line of the code shown in Figure 6.4 does exactly this and generates the appropriate value for the numerator. This new numerator value is then multiplied by –1 and divided by the estimated coefficient of the bid variable (i.e., _b[bid]). The mean WTP for the whole sample and the corresponding 95% confidence interval are obtained using the *ci* command.

Figure 6.4: Computing for Mean WTP by Generating Respondent-Specific WTPs

```
. predict numerator, xb

. replace numerator=numerator-_b[bid]*bid
(2,500 real changes made)

. gen wtp=-numerator/_b[bid]

. ci means wtp

 Variable |    Obs      Mean     Std. Err.      [95% Conf. Interval]
----------+-------------------------------------------------------
      wtp |  2,500   164.9238   .2272924      164.4781   165.3695
```

Source: Authors.

Finally, the third approach is to use a user-written program, *wtpcikr* (Wilner 2008). The command *wtpcikr* computes the mean and median WTP and the confidence interval using the Krinsky and Robb method.[30] Figure 6.5 shows the results of this user-written command. It is important to observe the following rules when using the *wtpcikr* command to derive the mean WTP:

(i) The bid variable should be the first variable after the dependent variable in the logit command.

[30] Krinsky and Robb uses a parametric bootstrap to estimate the confidence interval (see Jeanty [2008] for more details).

(ii) The order of independent variables in the logit regression should be the same as that in the *wtpcikr* command.

Figure 6.5: Deriving the Mean WTP Using the User-Written Command *wtpcikr*

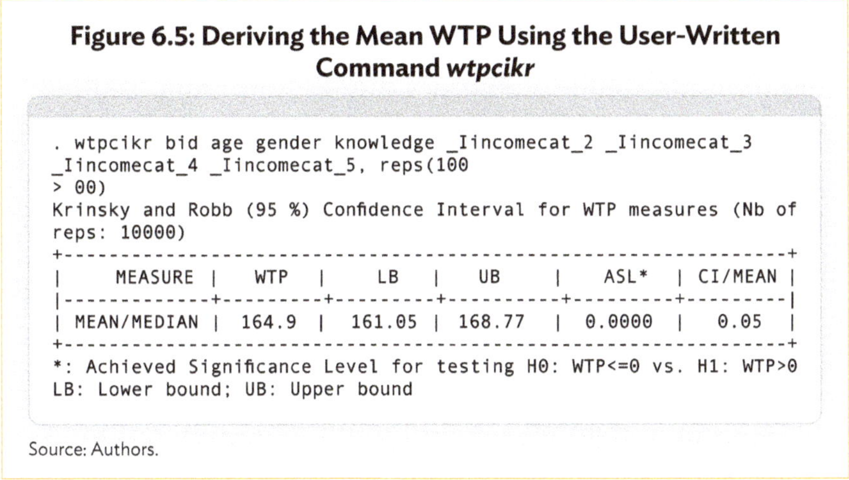

```
. wtpcikr bid age gender knowledge _Iincomecat_2 _Iincomecat_3
_Iincomecat_4 _Iincomecat_5, reps(100
> 00)
Krinsky and Robb (95 %) Confidence Interval for WTP measures (Nb of
reps: 10000)
+---------------------------------------------------------------------+
|     MEASURE |   WTP    |   LB     |   UB      |   ASL*    | CI/MEAN |
|-------------+----------+----------+-----------+-----------+---------|
| MEAN/MEDIAN |  164.9   |  161.05  |  168.77   |  0.0000   |   0.05  |
+---------------------------------------------------------------------+
*: Achieved Significance Level for testing H0: WTP<=0 vs. H1: WTP>0
LB: Lower bound; UB: Upper bound
```

Source: Authors.

Finally, note that the three different approaches produce the same mean WTP. The difference lies mainly in the range of the 95% confidence interval. If the mean WTP is the main interest of the study, then any of the three methods can be used. However, if the confidence interval is also a focus of the study, then the interval obtained through the Krinsky-Robb method is preferred.

Preparing Data from a Payment Card Elicitation Format

The parameters of the WTP function from a payment card elicitation format, which is described in Appendix 7, can be estimated using a variety of regression models. The choice of models will depend on the way the dependent variable is constructed from the respondent's chosen bid. In particular, the dependent variable can be either the interval bounded by b_k, and, b_{k+1}, the midpoint of this interval, the chosen bid or payment, b_k, itself, or treating the intervals as ordered categories. For example, if the respondent is to choose from the following set of bids or payments: 0, 50, 100, 150, 200, and 250, the values of the dependent variable can be constructed as shown in Table 6.1.

Table 6.1: Values of Constructed Dependent Variables for a Payment Card Elicitation Format

Chosen Payment/ Bid	Point Estimate (Bid)	Point Estimate (Mid-Point)	Interval Data		
			Lower Bound	Upper Bound	Category
0	0	25	– ∞	50	1
50	50	50	50	100	2
100	100	125	100	150	3
150	150	175	150	200	4
200	200	225	200	250	5
250	250	250	250	+ - ∞	6

Source: Authors.

The regressors or independent variables that can be used for the regressions are similar to those identified for the SBDC elicitation format. The notable change is that the bid (or more correctly the transformation of the bid variable, denoted as WTP') will now be the dependent variable in the regression models that will be used. Note that, in contrast, the bid level is part of the set of regressors for the SBDC elicitation format.

$$\log \text{WTP} = \beta_0 + \sum_{K} \beta_k X_k + \sum_{I} \beta_{Yi} Yi + \varepsilon$$

Estimation for a Payment Card Elicitation Format: Interval Data

Given the log-normal specification for the WTP function, the mean WTP can be derived using the following formula:

$$\text{mean } WTP = \exp\left(\beta_0 + \sum \beta_k X_k + \sum \beta_{Yi} Y_i + \sigma^2/2\right)$$

The variables for the lower and upper bound, corresponding to the fourth and fifth columns of Table 6.1, should be generated first, and the lower and upper bounds should be converted into log values before running the regression. The interval regression is ran using the *intreg* command of Stata. Figure 6.6 shows the results of the *intreg* command.

Figure 6.6: Interval Regression Commands and Results in Stata

```
. intreg lowbound uprbound age i.incomecat gender knowledge

Fitting constant-only model:

Iteration 0:   log likelihood = -4326.9064
Iteration 1:   log likelihood =  -3879.728
Iteration 2:   log likelihood = -3842.4408
Iteration 3:   log likelihood = -3842.4207
Iteration 4:   log likelihood = -3842.4207

Fitting full model:

Iteration 0:   log likelihood = -4309.8698
Iteration 1:   log likelihood = -3862.6068
Iteration 2:   log likelihood = -3826.1815
Iteration 3:   log likelihood = -3826.1642
Iteration 4:   log likelihood = -3826.1642

Interval regression                    Number of obs     =      2,500
                                       Uncensored        =          0
                                       Left-censored     =      1,109
                                       Right-censored    =         46
                                       Interval-cens.    =      1,345

                                       LR chi2(7)        =      32.51
Log likelihood = -3826.1642            Prob > chi2       =     0.0000

------------------------------------------------------------------
          | Coef      Std. Err.     z   P>|z|   [95% Conf. Interval]
----------+-------------------------------------------------------
age       | .0140058   0049981    2.80  0.005    .0042096   .0238019
          |
incomecat |
        2 | .0191561  .0810884    0.24  0.813   -.1397743   .1780865
        3 | .1643906  .0740075    2.22  0.026    .0193385   .3094427
        4 | .2005617  .0739357    2.71  0.007    0556503    .3454731
        5 |  .069343    .07421    0.93  0.350   -.0761059   .2147919
          |
gender    | .2037553  .0686817    2.97  0.003    .0691416    .338369
knowledge | .0103153  .0156774    0.66  0.511   -.0204119   .0410425
_cons     | 3.338809  .1869286   17.86  0.000    2.972435   3.705182
----------+-------------------------------------------------------
/lnsigma  |-.1091855  .0218446   -5.00  0.000   -.1520002  -.0663709
----------+-------------------------------------------------------
sigma     |   896564   0195851                   8589881    9357837
------------------------------------------------------------------
```

Source: Authors.

Presenting and Interpreting Results from the Interval Regression

The presentation of the interval regression results follows the minimum reporting requirements discussed earlier (Figure 6.7 shows the presentation of the results). The interpretation of the coefficients is different from that of the SBDC model in that the coefficients are the marginal effects of the variables. Hence, for the age variable, the results indicate that a 1-year increase in the age of the respondent increases, all else constant, the WTP by $0.014. For a binary variable like gender, the coefficient means that a male respondent's predicted WTP compared with a female respondent's predicted WTP is, on average, higher by $0.204.

Figure 6.7: Sample of Reporting Regression Results from Payment Card Data

Results of Interval Regression

Dependent Variable	Bid
Independent Variables	Coefficient
Constant/Intercept	3.339*** (0.187)[a]
Age	0.014** (0.005)
Gender (Male =1; Female=0)	0.204*** (0.069)
Knowledge	0.010 (0.016)
Income Categories:	
Income Category 2	0.019 (0.016)
Income Category 3	0.164** (0.074)
Income Category 4	0.200*** (0.074)
Income Category 5	0.069 (0.074)
Log-likelihood	-3826.164
Chi squared (7)	32.510
N	2500

*** = significant at 1%; ** = significant at 5%; * = significant at 10%.

[a] Standard errors in parentheses.

Source: Authors.

Deriving the WTP Estimates from a Payment Card Data

The mean WTP from the interval regression can be computed after running Stata's *intreg*. The WTP formula is described in Appendix 7. From the formula, $\widehat{\beta}'X$ can be generated using the *predict* command. On the other hand, σ, which is stored in Stata's memory as e(sigma), can be generated as a new variable. Figure 6.8 shows the series of commands to generate the mean WTP from the interval regression, WTP_int. The results and the 95% confidence interval that bounds this mean WTP are also shown in Figure 6.8.

Figure 6.8: Stata Commands to Generate the Mean WTP from the Interval Regression

```
. predict exb, xb

. scalar sigest=e(sigma)

. gen WTP_int=exp(exb+(sigest*sigest/2))

.
. ci means WTP_int

Variable  |  Obs        Mean       Std. Err.     [95% Conf. Interval]
----------+----------------------------------------------------------
WTP_int   |  2,500    91.21994    .2007802      90.82623    91.61366
```

Source: Authors.

Assessing the Validity of CV Findings

The CV method has been subjected to controversies and intense scrutiny especially in its ability to produce valid and reliable WTP estimates. Thus, validity and reliability checks should always be done while analyzing the CVM data. The information needed to conduct these assessments or checks should have been collected through the CV survey. In particular, this information is generated from a respondent's answers to debriefing or follow-up questions (see discussions regarding CV questionnaire design in Chapter 4).

Validity refers to the minimization of bias in the WTP estimates. Validity assessment is associated with finding evidence that the study measured what it was intended to. From an external evaluator's point of view, a good assessment of a CV study's validity is highly related to and facilitated by the detailed reporting found in a CV study.

Reliability, on the other hand, is the minimization of the variance of estimates across time and studies. It is synonymous to the reproducibility of the results of a CV study. It is related more to the evaluation of the methodology itself rather than the acceptability of the results of a particular study.

Validity Assessments

Content validity. Content validity tries to determine whether the survey instrument, particularly the CV scenario, induces the respondent to reveal true WTP values. A CV study is deemed to have high content validity if there is evidence that actions were taken to ensure that the CV scenario is consequential and incentive compatible. Thus, evidence of an adequately pretested (qualitative and quantitative) CV questionnaire is an indicator of content validity.

The frequency of protest votes also reveals how respondents react to the elements in the CV scenario, including the payment mechanism and institutional arrangements. Thus, evidence of accounting for protest behavior in the analysis and questionnaire design as well as the magnitude of protest behavior is indicative of the content validity of a CV study. The indicators of respondents' appreciation and understanding of the CV scenario and their perceived consequentiality of the scenario are also evidence of a CV study's content validity.

Convergent validity. This indicates the consistency of WTP estimates in comparison to alternative nonmarket valuation methods (such as revealed preference methods). It establishes the comparability of two valuation approaches in terms of having the same magnitude of bias (OECD 2018; Champ, Boyle, and Brown 2017). Carson et al. (2006) performed a meta-analysis of 83 valuation studies that used different methods to elicit WTP. He concluded that despite the hypothetical construct of the CV method, the derived WTP values are very similar to the estimates from revealed preference techniques,[31] with results also showing a high correlation between the two methods.

Construct validity. This refers to the consistency of CV results with predictions from economic theory, or what can also be referred to as theoretical validity. A CV study is deemed to produce construct valid

[31] OECD (2018) noted, however, that the narrow scope of revealed preference techniques in only providing use value estimates limits the applicability of convergent validity testing to quasi-public goods, as pure public goods cannot be analyzed similarly.

results if the results of the data analysis show that the WTP estimates have an inverse relationship with the bid level and a positive relationship with the income levels.[32] Another indicator of construct validity includes the sensitivity of WTP estimates to scope (part-whole bias) and whether WTA and WTP yield the same results when similar changes in the provision of goods or services are valued.

Criterion validity. This is the most direct way to check if WTP estimates from CV studies are valid, by comparing hypothetical values with the values obtained from simulated laboratory or field experiments that use real money—which is presumed to be the true measure of value. For example, auctioning off water filters or water purifiers leads to estimates of people's WTP for clean or better-quality water. This estimate can be compared with WTP estimates from a CVM analysis. Because real money and payments are involved, auctions are presumed to be devoid of hypothetical bias.

Reliability

The reliability criterion measures the stability of WTP measures over time such as the magnitude of variance in CV estimates (i.e., error dispersion) after repeated applications. The smaller the standard error, the more reliable the value estimates. A test-retest method is a common approach used to establish this. The CV survey is repeated at two different points in time either with the same respondents or with two samples drawn from the same sampling frame (i.e., between-subjects design).

Reliability tests are not often carried out or assessed in CVM applications since it is impractical to do repeat surveys. These tests often answer questions regarding the methodology itself rather than the results of an individual CVM study. However, the vast literature on CVM seems to unanimously concur with the conclusion that CV estimates are reliable (OECD 2018). However, it is important to recognize that values can change reasonably over time, and this in no way refutes the reliability criterion even if statistical equivalence cannot be established. Reviewing the test-retest contingent valuation literature, McConnell, Strand, and Valdes (1997) concluded that WTP values are stable over a 2-year period.

[32] This can be verified through a significant and negative sign of the regression coefficient of the bid variable and a significant and positive sign of the regression coefficient of the income variable.

CHAPTER 7

FUTURE DIRECTIONS FOR CVM PRACTICE

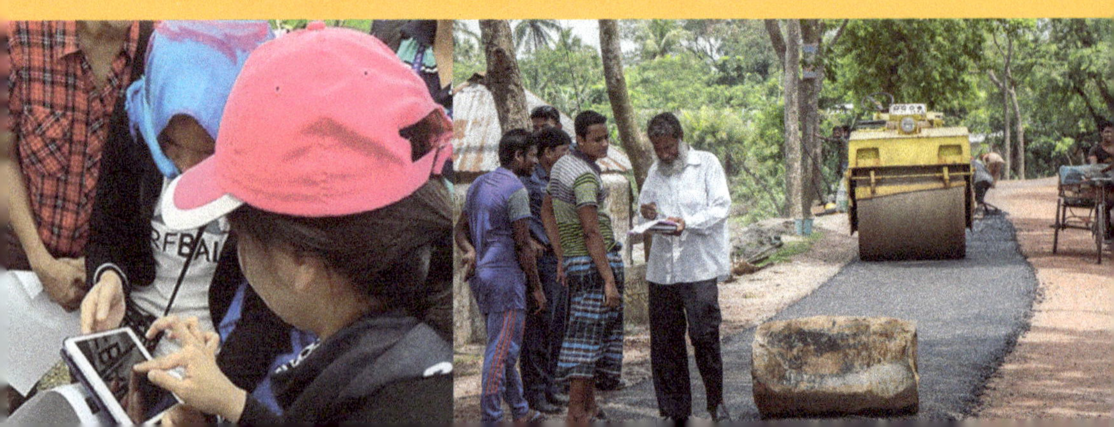

Key Messages:

- Recommended CVM practices have remained relatively stable over the past 3 decades, but progress has been made on measures that can mitigate bias.
- A core set of good practices can enable CVM to offer reliable estimates.
- As recognition of the importance of nonmarket benefits grows, the need for CVM will also expand.
- CVM creates an opportunity to better understand human motivations and behavior in project decision-making process.
- CVM is a tool to help inform project design.
- From a long-term perspective, well-implemented and compiled CVM studies can help to interface with other disciplines in ways that benefit both broader understanding of economics and the reliability of CVM practice.

This resource book has presented a review of the current practices on the use of the contingent valuation method (CVM). While the review represents the common current practices, the methodology is still evolving as researchers and practitioners respond to recurrent past and emerging criticisms against it. This final chapter highlights and summarizes the main lessons and takeaways from this review.

Summary of Good Practice

The National Oceanic and Atmospheric Administration (NOAA) Guidelines for CVM by Arrow et al. (1993) is a milestone that has guided practice in the field for many years. CVM guidelines have not changed much since then. The latest set of recommendations by Johnston et al. (2017) reiterated some of these guidelines and added information from academic literature to resolve controversies that arose from the earlier NOAA guidelines.

Most work on CVM practice has centered on developed countries; however, the practice is also increasing in developing countries. For Asia, Gunatilake et al. (2007) published guidance on CVM analysis in the water and sanitation sector. Minor changes to this material and other work by the author were incorporated in ADB (2013). Although aimed at a specific sector, ADB guidelines are broad enough to apply to CVM practice in general. A series of studies followed, demonstrating these best practices in water and sewerage projects and then later in valuing electricity improvements. Table 7.1 summarizes the different recommendations from these documents. Developments from the initial NOAA recommendations have largely emerged through additional bias-mitigating mechanisms, validity assessments, and new econometric models used in analyzing CVM data.

Improved bias-mitigating practices. These include the use of cheap talk scripts and other entreaties, provision point mechanisms, debriefing questions that detect protest and uncertainty, and mandatory payments. There has also been recent interest on debriefing or follow-up questions to assess perceived degree of consequentiality of the hypothetical CV scenario.

Validity assessments. At the minimum, content and construct validity should be demonstrated and documented. Content validity can be deduced through the documentation of procedures and activities performed in developing the CV scenario. Construct validity on the other hand is evaluated by comparing the results of the CVM analysis with economic theory. Gunatilake et al. (2007) identified these assessments as being important. These are also recommended areas for research as indicated in Table 7.1.

Econometric models. Models for analyzing CVM data have also expanded since the time of the NOAA panel. This is partly because WTP elicitation formats have also evolved, such as the increasing use of the multiple-bound dichotomous choice (or stochastic payment cards) as an alternative to the single-bounded dichotomous choice (SBDC) elicitation format. These developments were borne out of the impracticality of large sample sizes associated with SBDC.

Table 7.1: Recommended CVM Practices by Various Authors

CVM Stages	NOAA Panel (Arrow et al. 1993)	Gunatilake et al. (2007); ADB (2013)	Johnston et al. (2017)
Questionnaire Development	- Careful pretesting of CV questionnaire, including pretesting for interviewer effects and photographs - Accurate description of the program or policy - Use referendum voting elicitation format (i.e., dichotomous choice) and WTP instead of WTA - Respondents must be reminded of substitute commodities, such as other comparable natural resources or the future state of the same natural resource. This reminder should be introduced forcefully and directly before the main valuation question to ensure that respondents have the alternatives clearly in mind. - Respondents must be reminded that their willingness to pay for the environmental program in question would reduce their expenditure for private goods or other public goods. - Should have yes/no follow-ups after valuation questions (debriefing). - The survey should include a variety of other questions that help to interpret the responses to the primary valuation question (auxiliary questions). - Include checks on understanding and acceptance of scenario.	- Precise commodity definition informed by preparatory activities and FGDs - Close ended (referendum) format - Include socioeconomic profile of respondents, behavior related to the good being valued - Questionnaire should include debriefing questions - Focus group discussions (FGDs) and pretesting before finalization of instruments	- CV scenario should clearly define the baseline (or without-project) condition(s), the mechanism of change, and the change(s) to be valued and should elicit evidence that these pieces of information are understood, accepted, and viewed as credible by respondents. - Payment vehicle and amounts must be clearly stated (who pays, mandatory payment for incentive compatibility, frequency, and duration of payment). -Mandatory payment is preferred for incentive compatibility. Voluntary payment vehicles can be used but must be coupled with a provision point mechanism. - Payment vehicle should be selected to be realistic, credible, familiar, and binding for all respondents to as great an extent as possible and to ensure that payments are viewed as fixed and nonmalleable. - Decision context generally determines whether WTP or WTA is the most appropriate welfare measure from a conceptual perspective, but the final choice of welfare measure should be motivated by a combination of theory and empirical considerations, and the motivation for this choice should be explained. - A realistic decision rule that is binding on respondents should be selected. Referendum voting formats should be considered where plausible but are not always relevant to the choice context in question.

continued on next page

Table 7.1 (continued)

CVM Stages	**NOAA Panel** (Arrow et al. 1993)	**Gunatilake et al.** (2007); **ADB** (2013)	**Johnston et al.** (2017)
Questionnaire Development			- SBDC is preferred for its incentive compatibility properties when valuing public goods, but use of other formats is acceptable with adequate justification and documentation of use. - Purposeful auxiliary questions that enhance the validity of the SP study should be included. - Research into the use of ex-ante procedures to enhance validity (cheap talk, oath scripts, provision point mechanisms, etc.) are encouraged and their use is recommended. - Qualitative (FGDs, cognitive interview, etc.) and quantitative, i.e., piloting of the questionnaire should be done.
Survey Implementation	- Use of probability sampling with a total sample size of around 1,000 - Minimize nonresponses - Personal or face-to-face interview	- In-person or face-to-face interview - Stratified or cluster sampling with proper description of sampling frame and strategy together with replacement strategy - Adequate sample size based on size of population, number of CV scenarios, number of bids, number of anticipated split samples - Enumerator training is recommended	- Most appropriate mode of data collection is context specific and the rationale for the selected mode should be documented. - Random sampling from known sampling frame. - Contemporary approaches should be used to identify and mitigate nonresponse bias. But acknowledges that nonresponse bias cannot be solely inferred from response rates.

continued on next page

Table 7.1 (continued)

CVM Stages	**NOAA Panel** (Arrow et al. 1993)	**Gunatilake et al.** (2007); **ADB** (2013)	**Johnston et al.** (2017)
Data Analysis	- The final report should include summaries of willingness to pay broken down by categories (e.g., income, prior knowledge of the good, etc.) - Cross-tabulations of response to the primary valuation question with income, prior knowledge, attitudes toward environment, attitudes toward big business, etc. - Elimination of "protest zeros" in the sample	- Descriptive statistics of variables - Cross-tabulations by socioeconomic, geographic, and current use status for all important variables - Computation of mean WTP	- No one particular model or set of econometric models is recommended. Choice should be based on the unique characteristics of the data, hypothesis to be tested, and how estimates will be used for decision-making. Documentation of model selection and specification should be made explicit. - Analysis should allow for incorporation of observed and unobserved preference heterogeneity. - Data analysis should include the simplest, most parsimonious specifications with maintained hypotheses consistent with the basic axioms of choice (negative relationship with bids, positive relationship with income WTP a small fraction of gross income, and properties of the data. - Use of data from the supporting and debriefing questions should be accompanied by clear theoretical, survey design or empirical arguments explaining and justifying their use. - Reported welfare estimates should include at the minimum central tendency and dispersion. Transparency in welfare calculation methods. - Generalizability of the WTP estimates should be documented even if aggregation is not an objective. Potential users should have an idea of sample representativeness.

continued on next page

Table 7.1 (continued)

CVM Stages	NOAA Panel (Arrow et al. 1993)	Gunatilake et al. (2007); ADB (2013)	Johnston et al. (2017)
Validity Assessment	Findings are "unreliable" if - Nonresponse rate is lacking - Responsiveness to scope of change is lacking - Understanding of the tasks is lacking - Belief in (restoration) scenario is lacking - Yes or no votes are not followed up or explained with reference to cost and/or value of program	- CV responses and WTP estimates must be correlated with and comparable to indicators of demand for water supply and sanitation (WSS) revealed through coping, averting, and other "revealed preference" data whenever possible (convergent validity). - Results should be consistent with predictions of economic theory (construct validity).	- Analysis should include a set of core internal validity assessments, including formal tests of construct and evaluations of content validity. There is no unequivocal recommendation of what these tests are but recommend continued research. - Validity assessment should include study-specific design and analysis procedures and outcomes, as well as consideration of knowledge from the body of preceding research.
Reporting	- Every report of a CV study should make clear the definition of the population sampled, the sampling frame used, the sample size, the overall sample nonresponse rate and its components (e.g., refusals), and item nonresponse on all important questions. The report should also reproduce the exact wording and sequence of the questionnaire and of other communications to respondents (e.g., advance letters). All data from the study should be archived and made available to interested parties.	- Should provide adequate information on the preparatory activities to understand and make a judgment about the quality of the CV survey design.	- All studies fully document study design, implementation, analyses, and results.

CV = contingent valuation, CVM = contingent valuation method, FGD = focus group discussion, NOAA = National Oceanic and Atmospheric Administration, SBDC = single-bounded dichotomous choice, WTP = willingness to pay, WTA = willingness to accept.
Source: Authors.

Other recommendations, on the other hand, have remained consistent. Among these are the development of a consequential CV scenario that clearly defines the changes in the good being valued, mechanisms to achieve this change, and adequate pretesting and ground truthing in the field.

Some recommendations, especially those pertaining to survey practices are patterned after common best practices in field surveys. One of these is to have the sampling design follow basic statistical requirements of random sampling. Standard econometric estimation practices of using post estimation diagnostics (i.e., checking for goodness-of-fit and variable significance, testing alternative specifications) are also similar to all econometric applications.

Recent recommendations (i.e., Johnston et al. 2017) are visibly more flexible on elicitation formats. For example, while SBDC is still the preferred elicitation format for valuing public goods because of its incentive compatible properties, the general sentiment is to accommodate a wider set of elicitation formats and encourage more research into this area. Table 7.2 summarizes good practices drawing on more recent recommendations.

Future Directions

The importance of nonmarket goods and services is increasingly being recognized globally, particularly in the field of development. Environmental, health, and amenity benefits are no longer expected from environmental projects only, but increasingly so from investments in sectors ranging from transport to energy and urban development. For these benefits to be given due consideration, they must be quantified, and quantification often depends on stated preference methods, such as CVM.

This is not only an opportunity for CVM to help justify projects and inform project design. It is also an opportunity to help better understand human motivations and behavior in the process. CVM studies have in recent decades revealed puzzling paradoxes about human preferences, such as disparities between WTP and WTA, and how iteration and information framing can affect WTP. Initially regarded as CVM criticisms, these observations also motivated substantial work in the field of behavioral economics, leading to many experimental studies that explore the limits of bounded rationality (OECD 2018). In turn, behavioral economics has helped to inform CVM design, so as to ensure incentive compatibility and the validity of estimates, and progressive experimentation in CVM

Table 7.2: Recommended Good CVM Practices for Project Economic Analysis

Questionnaire Development/ Design
1. CV scenario should contain (a) Clear definition of the good or service being valued (b) A clear description of the baseline (without-project) conditions/attributes of the good or service and the changes in these conditions/attributes resulting from the program (c) Clear description of the mechanisms that will bring these changes and identification of the institutional actor/s
2. Use of mandatory payment vehicle
3. Incorporate cheap talk scripts in the questionnaire
4. Use a provision point rule or mechanism
5. Well-considered elicitation format and questions appropriate to the cultural context and sampling
6. Include debriefing questions that address or capture (a) Protest behavior (b) Uncertainty (c) Perception of consequentiality
7. Include auxiliary questions related to (a) Sociodemographic characteristics (b) Income (c) Knowledge and attitudes toward the good or service (d) Behavior related to the provision of the good or service being valued
8. Qualitative and quantitative pretesting of the initial questionnaire should always be done
Survey
1. Probability or random sampling either through stratified or clustered sampling should be done
2. Sample size should have adequate power and effect sizes
3. Enumerator training should be done
4. Document number of nonresponses
Data Analysis
1. Regression model should be appropriate for the data and elicitation format adopted
2. Regression model should include income and bid
3. Analysis of data should account or correct for protest behavior, uncertainty, and perceived consequentiality
Validity Assessment
1. At the minimum, assess and report construct and content validity of the study
Reporting
1. Report and document all decisions and activities related to questionnaire development, survey, data analysis, and validity tests.

Source: Authors.

administration has helped to further refine methodologies (Box 7.1 illustrates how ADB's CVM efforts can also do so). Ongoing and improved applications of CVM can help drive a virtuous cycle of interaction between environmental and behavioral economics, which can ultimately help to ensure that the importance of nonmarket goods and services is better recognized in investment planning.

Box 7.1: Potential Contributions of ADB to CVM Methodology Development

It is worthwhile to note that within a span of 4 years (2016–2020), the Asian Development Bank (ADB) has funded around 34 contingent valuation method (CVM) studies. These studies could have contributed substantially to the global practice of CVM in two possible ways. First, CVM in ADB has been repeatedly applied to common projects; had all these projects employed a consistent set of practices, results across these studies could have been compared. Comparison of results would have given a better understanding of not only the methodology but also of people's preferences for common nonmarketed goods and services, especially that of the environment. From a long-term perspective, if CVM studies are well implemented and compiled within a common sector, willingness-to-pay (WTP) values from actual ADB project investments may stand to be a more reliable and defensible source of valuation when applying the "benefit transfer method" on future ADB projects. Second, these studies could have moved beyond the traditional application of using WTP estimates for cost-benefit analysis. They could have, for instance, embedded experimental designs that can lead to an improved understanding of the gray areas of the methodology such as the effect of cognitive and behavioral biases on WTP estimates. In addition, the estimates could have also helped resolve long-standing controversies such as the nature and impacts of hypothetical bias in CV studies. ADB has much potential therefore to contribute to the global direction of the methodology itself while facilitating the analysis of the economic viability of development projects.

Source: Authors.

References

Aadland, D. and A. Caplan. 2006. Cheap Talk Reconsidered: New Evidence from CVM. *Journal of Economic Behavior & Organization.* 60 (4). pp. 562–578.

Aizaki, H., T. Nakatani, and K. Sato. 2015. *Stated Preference Methods Using R.* Taylor & Francis Group.

Alberini, A., K. Boyle, and M. Welsh. 2003. Analysis of Contingent Valuation Data with Multiple Bids and Response Options Allowing Respondents to Express Uncertainty. *Journal of Environmental Economics and Management.* 45. pp. 40–62.

Alberini, A. and J. R. Kahn. 2006. Chapter 20: Conclusions. In A. Alberini and J. R. Kahn, eds. *Handbook of Contingent Valuation.* Massachusetts: Edward Elgar Publishing.

Alpizar, F., F. Carlsson, and O. Johansson-Stenman. 2008. Does Context Matter More for Hypothetical than for Actual Contributions: Evidence from a Natural Field Experiment. *Experimental Economics.* 11. pp. 299–314.

Alston, R. M. and C. Nowell. 1996. Implementing the Voluntary Contribution Game: A Field Experiment. *Journal of Economic Behavior and Organization*. 31. pp. 357–68.

Ambrecht, J. 2014. Use Value of Cultural Experiences: A Comparison of Contingent Valuation and Travel Cost. *Tourism Management.* 42. pp. 141–148.

Ao, C. L., L. Zhou, Y. Jiao, and S. X. Wang. 2016. Influence of Initial Bid Number and Sample Size on the Double-Bounded Dichotomous Choice Contingent Valuation Method. *Acta Ecologica Sinica.* 36 (3). pp. 854–862.

Ardilla, S., R. Quiroga, and W. J. Vaughan. 1998. A Review of the Use of Contingent Valuation Methods in Project Analysis at the Inter-American Development Bank.

Arrow, K., R. Solow, P. R. Portney, E. E. Leamer, R. Radner, and H. Schuman. 1993. Report of the NOAA Panel on Contingent Valuation. Washington, DC: National Oceanic and Atmospheric Administration. https://sites.google.com/site/economiayambiente/PanelNOAA.pdf.

Asian Development Bank (ADB). 2013. *Cost-Benefit Analysis for Development: A Practical Guide*. Manila.

_______. 2017. *Guidelines for the Economic Analysis of Projects*. Manila

Azjen, I., T. C. Brown, and L. H. Rosenthal. 1996. Information Bias in Contingent Valuation: Effects of Personal Relevance, Quality of Information, and Motivational Orientation. *Journal of Environmental Economics and Management*. 30 (1). pp. 43–57.

Bateman, I. J., R. T. Carson, B. Day, M. Hanemann, N. Hanley, T. Hett, M. Jones-Lee, G. Loomes, S. Mourato, E. Ozdemigrolu, D. W. Pearce, R. Sudgen, and J. Swanson. 2002. *Economic Valuation with Stated Preference Techniques: A Manual*. Cheltenham, United Kingdom: Edward Elgar.

Ben-Akiva, M. and S. R. Lerman. 1985. *Discrete Choice Analysis: Theory and Application to Travel Demand*. Cambridge, Massachusetts: MIT Press.

Bergstrom, J. C., J. R. Stoll, and A. Randall. 1989. Information Effects in Contingent Markets. *American Journal of Agricultural Economics*. 71 (3). pp. 685–691.

Blomquist, G. C. and J. C. Whitehead. 1998. Resource Quality Information and Validity of Willingness to Pay in Contingent Valuation. *Resource and Energy Economics*. 20 (2). Elsevier. pp. 179–196. https://libres.uncg.edu/ir/asu/f/Whitehead_John_1998_Resource_quality_information.pdf.

Blumenschein, K., G. C. Blomquist, M. Johannesson, N. Horn, and P. Freeman. 2008. Eliciting Willingness to Pay without Bias: Evidence from a Field Experiment. *The Economic Journal*. 118 (1). pp. 114–137.

Bockstael, N. and K. E. McConnell. 2007. *Environmental and Resource Valuation with Revealed Preferences: A Theoretical Guide to Empirical Models*. The Netherlands: Springer.

Böheim, R. and S. P. Jenkins. 2006. A Comparison of Current and Annual Measures of Income in the British Household Panel Survey. *Journal of Official Statistics*. 22. pp. 733–758.

Boutwell, J. and J. Westra. 2013. Benefit Transfer: A Review of Methodologies and Challenges. *MDPI*. 2. pp. 517–527.

Boyd, J. and A. Krupnick. 2009. The Definition and Choice of Environmental Commodities for Non-Market Valuation. RFF Discussion Paper. 09–35. Washington, DC: Resources for the Future.

Boyd, J., P. Ringold, A. Krupnick, R. J. Johnston, M. A. Weber, and K. Hall. 2016. Ecosystem Services Indicators: Improving the Linkage between Biophysical and Economic Analyses. *International Review of Environmental and Resource Economics*. 8 (3–4). pp. 359–443.

Boyle, K. J., R. Bishop, D. Hellerstein, M. P. Welsh, M. C. Ahearn, A. Laughland, J. Charbonneau, and R. O'Conner. 1998. Test of Scope in Contingent Valuation Studies: Are the Numbers for the Birds. In paper presented at the World Congress of Environmental and Resource Economists (AERE/EAERE). Venice, Italy. 25–27 June.

Boyle, K. J. 2003. Contingent Valuation in Practice. In P. A. Champ, K. J. Boyle, and T. C. Brown, eds. *A Primer on Non-Market Valuation*. New York: Springer Science+Business Media.

Brander, L. 2015. *Guidance Manual on Value Transfer Methods for Ecosystem Service*. Nairobi: United Nations Environment Programme.

Brown, T. C., I. Ajzen, and D. Hrubes. 2003. Further Tests of Entreaties to Avoid Hypothetical Bias in Referendum Contingent Valuation. *Journal of Environmental Economics and Management*. 46 (2). pp. 353–361.

Calderon, M., L. Camacho, M. Carandang, J. Dizon, L. Rebugio, and N. Tolentino. 2005. A Water User Fee for Households in Metro Manila, Philippines. *Economy and Environment Program for Southeast Asia (EEPSEA) Working Paper*. No. 2005-RR2. Singapore: EEPSEA.

Cameron, T. A. and D. D. Huppert. 1989. OLS versus ML Estimation of Non-market Resource Values with Payment Card Interval Data. *Journal of Environmental Economics and Management*. 17. pp. 230–46.

Cameron, T. A. 1992. Combining Contingent Valuation and Travel Cost Data for the Valuation of Nonmarket Goods. *Land Economics*. 68 (3). pp. 302–17.

Carson, R. T. and W. M. Hanemann. 2005. Chapter 17: Contingent Valuation. In K.-G. Mäler and J. R. Vincent, eds. *Handbook of Environmental Economics, Volume 2*. Elsevier.

Carson, R. T. and R. C. Mitchell. 1995. Sequencing and Nesting in Contingent Valuation Surveys. *Journal of Environmental Economics and Management*. 28 (2). pp. 155–173.

Carson, R. T., N. E. Flores, K. M. Martin, and J. L. Wright. 1996. Contingent Valuation and Revealed Preference Methodologies: Comparing the Estimates for Quasi-Public Goods. *Land Economics*. 72 (1). pp. 80–99.

Carson, R. T., T. Groves, and M. J. Machina. 1997. Stated Preference Questions: Context and Optimal Response. Paper presented at the National Science Foundation Preference Elicitation Symposium. University of California, Berkeley.

Carson, R. T., T. Groves, and M. Machina. 1999. Incentive and Informational Properties of Preferences Questions. Plenary Address, European Association of Environmental and Resource Economists. Oslo, Norway.

Carson, R. T. 2000. Contingent Valuation: A User's Guide. Environmental Science and Technology. 34 (8). pp. 1413–1418. https://pubs.acs.org/doi/10.1021/es990728j.

Carson, R. T., N. E. Flores, and N. F. Meade. 2001. Contingent Valuation: Controversies and Evidence. *Environmental and Resource Economics*. 19 (1). pp. 173–210.

Carson, R. T. and T. Groves. 2007. Incentive and Informational Properties of Preference Questions. *Environmental and Resource Economics*. 37 (1). pp. 181–210.

Carson, K. S., S. M. Chilton, and W. G. Hutchinson. 2009. Necessary Conditions for Demand Revelation in Double Referenda. *Journal of Environmental Economics and Management*. 57 (2). pp. 219–25.

Carson, R. T. and J. J. Louviere. 2011. A Common Nomenclature for Stated Preference Elicitation Approaches. *Environmental and Resource Economics*. 49 (4). pp. 539–559.

Carson, R. T., T. Groves, and J. A. List. 2014. Consequentiality: A Theoretical and Experimental Exploration of a Single Binary Choice. *Journal of the Association of Environmental and Resource Economists*. 1 (1). pp. 171–207.

Champ, P. A., R. C. Bishop, T. C. Brown, and D. W. McCollum. 1997. Using Donation Mechanisms to Value Nonuse Benefits from Public Goods. *Journal of Environmental Economics and Management*. 33 (2). pp. 151–162.

Champ, P. A., E. F. Nicholas, T. C. Brown, and J. Chivers. 2002. Contingent Valuation and Incentives. *Land Economics.* 78 (4). pp. 591–604.

Champ, P. A. 2003. Collecting Survey Data for Nonmarket Valuation. In P. A. Champ, K. J. Boyle, and T. C. Bron, eds. *A Primer on Nonmarket Valuation*. Kluwer Academic Publishers.

Champ, P. A. and R. C. Bishop. 2006. Is the Willingness to Pay for Public Goods Sensitive to Elicitation Format?. *Land Economics*. 82 (2). pp. 162–173.

Champ, P., R. Moore, and R. C. Bishop. 2009. A Comparison of Approaches to Mitigate Hypothetical Bias. *Agricultural and Resource Economics Review.* 38 (2). pp. 166–180.

Champ, P., K. J. Boyle, and T. C. Brown, eds. 2017. *A Primer on Nonmarket Valuation.* 2nd edition. The Netherlands: Springer Nature.

Choynowski, P. 2002. Measuring Willingness to Pay for Electricity. *ERD Technical Note Series*. No. 3. Manila: ADB.

Christantoni, M. and D. Damigos. 2018. Individual Contributions, Provision Point Mechanisms and Project Cost Information Effects on Contingent Values: Findings from a Field Validity Test. *Science of the Total Environment.* 624. pp. 628–637.

Christie, M. 2007. An Examination of the Disparity between Hypothetical and Actual Willingness to Pay Using the Contingent Valuation Method: The Case of Red Kite Conservation in the United Kingdom. *Canadian Journal of Agricultural Economics.* 55 (2). pp. 159–169.

Cummings, R. G., D. S. Brookshire, and W. D. Schulze, eds. 1986. *Valuing Environmental Goods—An Assessment of the Contingent Valuation Method.* Totowa, NJ: Roman and Allanheld.

Cummings, R. G., G. W. Harrison, and E. E. Rutström. 1995. Homegrown Values and Hypothetical Surveys: Is the Dichotomous Choice Approach Incentive-Compatible. *American Economic Review*. 85 (1). pp. 260–266.

Cummings, R. G., S. Elliott, G. W. Harrison, and J. Murphy. 1997. Are Hypothetical Referenda Incentive Compatible? *Journal of Political Economy*. 105 (3). pp. 609–621.

Cummings, R. G. and L. O. Taylor. 1999. Unbiased Value Estimates for Environmental Goods: A Cheap Talk Design for the Contingent Valuation Method. *American Economic Review*. 89 (3). pp. 649–665.

Davern, M., H. Rodin, T. Beebe, and K. Thiede Call. 2005. The Effect of Income Question Design in Health Surveys on Family Income, Poverty and Eligibility Estimates. *Health Services Research*. October. pp. 1534–1552.

De-Magistris, T., F. Akaichi, and K. Ben Youssef. 2016. Testing the Effectiveness of the Oath Script in Reducing the Hypothetical Bias in the Contingent Valuation Method. *Agricultural Economics – Czech*. 62. pp. 378–384.

Desvousges, W. H. and V. K. Smith. 1988. Focus Groups and Risk Communication: The "Science" of Listening to Data. *Risk Analysis*. 8 (4). pp. 479–84.

Ehmke, M. D., J. L. Lusk, and J. A. List. 2008. Is Hypothetical Bias a Universal Phenomenon? A Multinational Investigation. *Land Economics*. 84 (3). pp. 489–500.

Rabiee, F. 2004. Focus Group Interview and Data Analysis. *Proceedings of the Nutrition Society*. 63 (4). pp. 655–60.

Flores, N. E. and R. T Carson. 1997. The Relationship Between the Income Elasticities of Demand and Willingness to Pay. *Journal of Environmental Economics and Management*. 33. pp. 287–295.

Flores, N. E. 2003. Conceptual Framework for Nonmarket Valuation. In Champ, P., Boyle, K. and T. Brown, eds. 2003. *Primer on Non-Market Valuation*. Kluwer Academic Publishing.

Freeman, A. M. 2003. Economic Valuation: What and Why. In Champ, P., K. Boyle, and T. Brown, eds. 2003. *Primer on Non-Market Valuation*. Kluwer Academic Publishing.

Freitas, H., M. Oliviera, M. Jenkins, and O. Popjoy. 1998. The Focus Group, A Qualitative Research Method. *ISRC Working Paper*. No. 010298. p. 22.

Georgiou, S., H. Langford, I. J. Bateman, and R. K. Turner. 1998. Determinants of Individuals' Willingness to Pay for Perceived Reductions in Environmental Health Risks: A Case Study of Bathing Water Quality. *Environment and Planning A: Economy and Space*. 30 (4). pp. 577–594.

Groothuis, P. A. and J. C. Whitehead. 2009. The Provision Point Mechanism and Scenario Rejection in Contingent Valuation. *Agricultural and Resource Economics Review*. 38 (2). pp. 271–280.

Groves, R. M., F. J. Fowler, Jr., M. P. Couper, J. M. Lepkowski, E. Singer, and R. Tourangea. 2009. *Survey Methodology*. Hoboken, NJ: Wiley.

Gunatilake, H., J. Yang, S. Pattanayak, and C. van den Berg. 2006. Willingness-to-Pay and Design of Water Supply and Sanitation Projects: A Case Study. *ERD Technical Note Series*. No. 19. Manila: ADB.

Gunatilake, H., J. Yang, S. Pattanayak, and K. Choe. 2007. Good Practices for Estimating Reliable Willingness to Pay Values in the Water and Sanitation Sector. *ERD Technical Note Series*. No. 23. Manila: ADB.

Gunatilake, H. and M. Tachiri. 2014. Willingness to Pay and Inclusive Tariff Designs for Improved Water Supply Services in Urban Bangladesh. *Journal of Sustainable Development*. 7 (5). pp. 212–230.

Guzman, R. M. and C. D. Kolstad. 2007. Researching Preferences, Valuation, and Hypothetical Bias. *Environmental and Resource Economics*. 37 (3). pp. 465–487.

Haab, T. C. and K. E. McConnell. 2002. *Valuing Environmental and Natural Resources: The Econometrics of Non-Market Valuation*. London: Edward Elgar Publishing Ltd. UK.

Hanley, N., S. Mourato, and R. E. Wright. Choice Modelling Approaches: A Superior Alternative for Environmental Valuation? *Journal of Economic Surveys*. 15 (3). pp. 435–462.

Hanemann, W. M. and B. Kanninen. 2001. The Statistical Analysis of Discrete Response CV Data. In I. J. Bateman and K. G. Willis, eds. 2001. *Valuing Environmental Preferences: Theory, and Practice of the Contingent Valuation Method in the US, EU, and Developing Countries*. Oxford University Press.

Hanxiao, W. and B. Qin. 2019. An Experimental Test of the Solemn Oath in Eliciting Sincere Preferences. MPRA Paper 95913. University Library of Munich, Germany.

Harrison, G. W. 2006. Making Choice Studies Incentive Compatible. In B. J. Kanninen, ed. *Valuing Environmental Amenities Using Stated Choice Studies*. New York: Springer.

Hausman, J. 2012. Contingent Valuation: From Dubious to Hopeless. *Journal of Economic Perspectives*. 26 (4). pp. 43–56.

Hensher, D. A., J. M. Rose, and W. H. Greene. 2005. *Applied Choice Analysis: A Primer*. New York: Cambridge University Press.

Herath, G. and J. Kennedy. 2004. Estimating the Economic Value of Mount Buffalo National Park with the Travel Cost and Contingent Valuation Models. *Tourism Economics.* 10 (1). pp. 63–78. https://doi.org/10.5367/000000004773166529.

Hoehn, J. P. and A. Randall. 2002. The Effect of Resource Quality Information on Resource Injury Perceptions and Contingent Values. *Resource and Energy Economics.* 24 (1–2). pp. 13–31. https://doi.org/10.1016/S0928-7655(01)00051-3.

Hutchinson, W. G. and S. M. Chilton. 1999. Do Focus Groups Contribute Anything to the Contingent Valuation Process? *Journal of Economic Psychology.* 20 (4). pp. 465–83.

Iarossi, G. 2006. *The Power of Survey Design: A User's Guide for Managing Surveys, Interpreting Results, and influencing Respondents.* Washington, DC: World Bank.

Ivehammar, P. 2009. The Payment Vehicle Used in CV Studies of Environmental Goods Does Matter. *Journal of Agricultural and Resource Economics.* 34 (3). pp. 450–63.

Jacquemet, N., R. V. Joule, S. Luchini, and J. F. Shogren. 2009. Preference Elicitation under Oath. *CES Working Paper.* No. 43. Paris: Université Panthéon-Sorbonne.

Jeanty, P. W. 2007. Constructing Krinsky and Robb Confidence Interval for Mean and Median WTP Using Stata. North American Stata Users' Group Meetings 2007. 8. Stata Users Group.

Jeanty, P. W. 2008. WTPCIKR: Stata Module to Estimate Krinsky and Robb Confidence Intervals for Mean and Median Willingness to Pay. *Statistical Software Components.* S456965. Boston College Department of Economics. https://ideas.repec.org/c/boc/bocode/s456965.html.

Johannesson, M., G. C. Blomquist, K. Blumenschein, P. O. Johansson, B. Liljas, and R. M. O'Connor. 1999. Calibrating Hypothetical Willingness to Pay Responses. *Journal of Risk and Uncertainty.* 18 (1). pp. 21–32.

Johnston, R. J., T. F. Weaver, L. A. Smith, and S. K. Swallow. 1995. Contingent Valuation Focus Groups: Insights from Ethnographic Interview Techniques. *Agricultural and Resource Economics Review.* 24. pp. 56–69.

Johnston, R. J. 2006. Is Hypothetical Bias Universal? Validating Contingent Valuation Response Using a Binding Public Referendum. *Journal of Environmental Economics and Management.* 52 (1). pp. 469–81.

Johnston, R., K. Boyle, W. Adamowicz, J. Bennett, R. Brouwer, T. A. Cameron, W. M. Hanemann, N. Hanley, M. Ryan, R. Scarpa, R. Tourangeau, and C. Vossler. 2017. Contemporary Guidance for Stated Preference Studies. *Journal of the Association of Environmental and Resource Economists*. 4 (2). pp. 319–405.

Jorgensen, B. S. 1999. Focus Groups on the Contingent Valuation Process: A Real Contribution or Missed Opportunity. *Journal of Economic Psychology*. 20 (4). pp. 85–89.

Kahneman, D. 1986. Comments on the Contingent Valuation Method. In R. G. Cummings, D. S. Brookshire, and W. D. Schulze, eds. *Valuing Environmental Goods: A State of the Arts Assessment of the Contingent Valuation Method*. Roweman and Allanheld, Totowa.

Kahneman, D., J. Knetsch, and R. Thaler. 1990. Experimental Tests of the Endowment Effect and the Coase Theorem. *Journal of Political Economy*. 98 (6). pp. 1325–1348.

Kanninen, B. 1995. Bias in Discrete Response Contingent Valuation. *Journal of Environmental Economics and Management*. 28 (1). pp. 114–125.

Khun, U. 2019. Measurement of Income in Surveys. *FORS Guide No. 02, Version 1.0*. Lausanne: Swiss Centre of Expertise in the Social Sciences FORS. doi:10.24449/FG-2019-00002.

Kim, S. and T. C. Haab. 2004. Revisiting Bid Design Issues in Contingent Valuation. Unpublished manuscript downloaded from https://core.ac.uk/reader/6679041 (accessed 19 November 2021).

Kling, C. L. 1997. The Gains from Combining Travel Cost and Contingent Valuation Data to Value Nonmarket Goods. *Land Economics*. 73 (3). pp. 428–439.

Koeml, D. and X. Yu. 2020. Choice Experiments in Non-Market Value Analysis: Some Methodological Issues. *Forestry Economics Review*. 2 (1). pp. 3–31.

Kotchen, M. J. and S. D. Reiling. 2000. Environmental Attitudes, Motivations, and Contingent Valuation of Nonuse Values: A Case Study Involving Endangered Species. *Ecological Economics*. 32 (1). pp. 93–107.

Krueger, R. A. 1994. *Focus Groups: A Practical Guide for Applied Research*. Thousand Oaks, CA: Sage Publications Inc.

Krupnick, A. and W. L. Adamowicz. 2006. Supporting Questions in Stated-Choice Studies. In B. J. Kanninen, ed. *Valuing Environmental Amenities Using Stated Choice Studies*. New York: Springer.

Krutilla, J. V. 1967. Conservation Reconsidered. *The American Economic Review*. 57 (4). pp. 777–786.

Landry, C. E. and J. A. List. 2007. Using Ex Ante Approach to Obtain Credible Signals for Value in Contingent Markets: Evidence from the Field. *American Journal of Agricultural Economics*. 89 (2). pp. 420–429.

Lauria, D. T., D. Whittington, K. Choe, C. Turingan, and V. Abad. 2001. Household Demand for Improved Sanitation Services: A Case Study of Calamba, the Philippines. In I. J. Bateman and K. G. Willis, eds. 2001. *Valuing Environmental Preferences: Theory, and Practice of the Contingent Valuation Method in the US, EU, and Developing Countries*. Oxford University Press.

List, J. A. 2001. Do Explicit Warnings Eliminate the Hypothetical Bias in Elicitation Procedures? Evidence from Field Auctions for Sports Cards. *American Economic Review.* 91 (5). pp. 1498–1507.

List, J. A., R. P. Berrens, A. K. Bohara, and J. Kerkvliet. 2004. Examining the Role of Social Isolation on Stated Preferences. *American Economic Review*. 94 (3). pp. 741–752.

Little, J. and R. Berrens. 2004. Explaining Disparities between Actual and Hypothetical Stated Values: Further Investigation Using Meta-analysis. *Economics Bulletin*. 3 (6). pp. 1–13.

Lloyd-Smith, P., E. Zawojska, and W. Adamiwicz. 2018. Moving Beyond the Contingent Valuation Versus Choice Experiment Debate – Presentation Effects in Stated Preference. *University of Warsaw Faculty of Economic Sciences Working Paper.* No. 14/2018.

Loomis, J., A. Gonzalez-Caban, and R. Gregory. 1994. Do Reminders of Substitutes and Budget Constraints Influence Contingent Valuation Estimates? *Land Economics*. 70 (4). pp. 499–506.

Lunt, P. 1999. Comments on Chilton and Hutchinson: Beyond Measurement Issues in the Focus Group Method. *Journal of Economic Psychology.* 20. pp. 491–94.

Lusk, J. L. 2003. Effects of Cheap Talk on Consumer Willingness-to-Pay for Golden Rice. *American Journal of Agricultural Economics*. 85 (4). pp. 840–856.

McConnell, K., I. E. Strand, and S. Valdes. 1997. Testing Temporal Reliability and Carry-Over Effect: The Role of Correlated Responses in Test-Retest Reliability Studies. *Environmental and Resource Economics*. 12. pp. 357–374. http://dx.doi.org/10.1023/A:1008264922331.

Mitchell, R. C. and R. T. Carson. 1989. Using Surveys to Value Public Goods: The Contingent Valuation Method. Washington, DC: Resources for the Future.

Mitchell, R. C. and R. T. Carson. 1995. Current Issues in the Design, Administration, and Analysis of Contingent Valuation Surveys. In P. Johansson, B. Kristrom, and K. Maler, eds. *Current Issues in Environmental Economics*. Manchester: Manchester University Press.

Morrison, M. D., R. K. Blamey, and J. W. Bennett. 2000. Minimizing Payment Vehicle Bias in Contingent Valuation Studies. *Environmental and Resource Economics*. 16. pp. 407–422. https://ideas.repec.org/a/kap/enreec/v16y2000i4p407-422.html.

Morrison, M. and T. C. Brown. 2009. Testing the Effectiveness of Certainty Scales, Cheap Talk, and Dissonance-Minimization in Reducing Hypothetical Bias in Contingent Valuation Studies. *Environmental and Resource Economics*. 44 (3). pp. 307–326

Murphy, J. J., T. Stevens, and D. Weatherhead. 2005. Is Cheap Talk Effective in Eliminating Hypothetical Bias in a Provision Point Mechanism? *Environmental and Resource Economics*. 30. pp. 327–343.

Nam, P. K. and T. V. H. Son. 2005. Recreational Value of the Coral Surrounding the Hon Mun Islands in Vietnam: A Travel Cost and Contingent Valuation Study. In M. Ahmed, C. K. Chong, and H. Cesar, eds. 2005. *Economic Valuation and Policy Priorities for Sustainable Management of Coral Reefs.* . Penang, Malaysia: WorldFish Center.

Newbold, S., R. D. Simpson, D. Mathew Massey, M. T. Heberling, W. Wheeler, J. Corona, and J. Hewitt. 2018. Benefit Transfer Challenges: Perspective from U.S. Practitioners. *Environmental and Resource Economics*. 69 (3). pp. 467–481. doi:10.1007/s10640-017-0207-7.

Nunes, P.A.L.D. and P. Nijkamp. 2006. Contingent Valuation Method. In M. Deakin, G. Mitchell, P. Nijkamp, and R. Vreeker, eds. *Sustainable Urban Development (Volume 2): The Environmental Assessment Methods*. UK: Routledge.

Organisation for Economic Co-operation and Development (OECD). 2018. *Cost-Benefit Analysis and the Environment: Further Developments and Policy Use*. Paris: OECD Publishing.

Pattanayak, S., C. van den Berg, J. Yang, and G. van Houtven. 2006. The Use of Willingness to Pay Experiments: Estimating Demand for Piped Water Connections in Sri Lanka. *World Bank Policy Research Working Paper*. No. 3818. Washington, DC: World Bank.

Pearce, D., D. Whittington, S. Georgiou, and D. 1994. *Project and Policy Appraisal: Integrating Economics and Environment.* Paris: OECD.

Pearce, D. and E. Ozdemigrolu. 2002. *Economic Valuation with Stated Preference Techniques*. London: Department of Transportation, Local Governance, and the Regions.

Pearce, D., G. Atkinson, and S. Mourato. 2006. *Cost-Benefit Analysis and the Environment.* Paris: OECD Publishing. https://doi.org/10.1787/9789264010055-7-en.

Perman, R., Y. Ma, J. McGilvray, and M. Common. 2003. *Natural Resource and Environmental Economics 3rd Edition*. Pearson Education Limited.

Poe, G. L., J. E. Clark, D. Rondeau, and W. D. Schulze. 2002. Provision Point Mechanisms and Field Validity Tests of Contingent Valuation. *Environmental and Resource Economics.* 23. pp. 105–31.

Powe, N. A. 2007. *Redesigning Environmental Valuation: Mixing Methods with Stated Preference Techniques*. Cheltenham: Edward Elgar.

Ready, R. C., M. C. Berger, and G. C. Blomquist. 1997. Measuring Amenity Benefits from Farmland: Hedonic Pricing vs. Contingent Valuation. *Growth and Change.* 28. pp. 438– 458.

Rondeau, D., W. D. Schulze, and G. L. Poe. 1999. Voluntary Revelation of the Demand for Public Goods Using a Provision Point Mechanism. *Journal of Public Economics.* 72. pp. 455–70.

Rose, J. M. and M. C. J. Bliemer. 2013. Sample Size Requirements for Stated Choice Experiments. *Transportation*. 40. pp. 1021–41.

Rose, S. K., J. Clark, L. P. Gregory, D. Rondeau, and W. D. Schulze. 2002. The Private Provision of Public Goods: Tests of a Provision Point Mechanism for Funding Green Power Programs. *Resource and Energy Economics*. 24. pp. 131–55.

Smith, V. K. 2007. Judging Quality. In B. Kanninen, ed. *Valuing Environmental Amenities Using Stated Choice Studies: A Commonsense Approach to Theory and Practice*. Dordrecht, The Netherlands: Springer.

Stevens, T. H., M. Tabatabaei, and D. Lass. 2013. Oaths and Hypothetical Bias. *Journal of Environmental Management*. 127. pp. 135–141.

Subade, R. F. 2007. Mechanisms to Capture Economic Values of Marine Biodiversity: The Case of Tubbataha Reefs UNESCO World Heritage Site, Philippines. *Marine Policy*. 31 (2). pp. 135–142.

Svedsäter, H. 2000. Contingent Valuation of Global Environmental Resources: A Test of Perfect and Regular Embedding. *Journal of Economic Psychology*. 21. pp. 605–623.

Tidwell, J. B. 2020. Users Are Willing to Pay for Sanitation, But Not as Much as They Say: Empirical Results and Methodological Comparisons of Willingness to Pay for Peri-urban Sanitation in Lusaka, Zambia Using Contingent Valuation, Discrete Choice Experiments, and Hedonic Pricing. *Journal of Water, Sanitation and Hygiene Development.* 10 (4). pp. 756–767.

United Nations Department of Economic and Social Affairs (UNDESA). 2005. *Household Sample Surveys in Developing and Transition Countries.* New York.

Vaughan, W. J. and A. H. Darling. 2000. The Optimal Sample Size for Contingent Valuation Surveys: Applications to Project Analysis. *IADB Sustainable Development Department Technical Papers Series.* No. ENV-136. Washington, DC: Inter-American Development Bank.

Veisten, K. 2007. Contingent Valuation Controversies: Philosophic Debates about Economic Theory. *Journal of Socioeconomics.* 36 (2). pp. 204–232.

Vossler, C. A. and J. Kerkvliet. 2003. A Criterion Validity Test of the Contingent Valuation Method: Comparing Hypothetical and Actual Voting Behavior for a Public Referendum. *Journal of Environmental Economics and Management.* 45. pp. 631–49.

Wang, H. and D. Whittington. 2005. Measuring Individuals' Valuation Distributions Using a Stochastic Payment Card Approach. *Ecological Economics* (55). pp. 143–154.

Welsh, M. P. and G. L. Poe. 1998. Elicitation Effects in Contingent Valuation: Comparison to a Multiple Bound Discrete Choice Approach. *Journal of Environmental Economics and Management.* 36. pp. 170–185.

Whitehead J. C. 2006. A Practitioner's Primer on the Contingent Valuation Method. In A. Alberini and J. R. Kahn, eds. *Handbook on Contingent Valuation.* UK: Edward Elgar Publishing.

Whittington, D. 1996. Administering Contingent Valuation Surveys in Developing Countries. Special Paper for the Economy and Environment Program for Southeast Asia (EEPSEA). Singapore.

Whittington, D. 1998. Administering Contingent Valuation Surveys in Developing Countries. *World Development.* 26. pp. 21–30.

Whittington, D. 2002. Improving the Performance of Contingent Valuation Studies in Developing Countries. *Environmental and Resource Economics*. 22 (1). pp. 323–367.

Whittington, D. 2004. Ethical Issues with Contingent Valuation Surveys in Developing Countries: A Note on Informed Consent and Other Concerns. *Environmental and Resource Economics*. 28. pp. 507–515.

Whittington, D. 2010. What Have We Learned from 20 Years of Stated Preference Research in Less Developed Countries? *Annual Review of Resource Economics*. 2 (1). pp. 209–236.

World Health Organization (WHO). 2012. *How to Conduct a Discrete Choice Experiment for Health Workforce Requirement and Retention in Remote and Rural Areas: A User Guide with Case Studies.* Geneva: WHO Press.

Zhongmin, X., C. Guodong, Z. Zhiqiang, S. Zhiyong, and J. Loomis. 2003. Applying Contingent Valuation in China to Measure the Total Economic Value of Restoring Ecosystem Services in Ejina Region. *Ecological Economics.* 44. pp. 345–358.

Glossary

Auxiliary questions are questions in a contingent valuation (CV) questionnaire that aim to capture information that can help explain respondents' stated willingness to pay.

Benefit transfer method refers to the use of previously established unit values of benefits that were estimated for study sites with similar characteristics as the proposed project site.

Bequest value is the utility derived from bequeathing environmental goods and services to future generations.

Bid distribution contains the range and levels of bids within this range.

Cheap talk script is a statement in the CV questionnaire reminding the respondent of commonly observed behaviors when people are confronted with a hypothetical scenario. It also contains reminders of the respondent's income constraint and the presence of alternative or substitutes to the good or service being valued.

Choice modeling is a type of stated preference valuation method. Like contingent valuation method, it is a survey-based approach to elicit a sample's willingness to pay for nonmarketed goods and services used and produced by a program or project. CM is an attribute-based stated choice method. The choice task of respondents in CM involves choosing among different descriptions of the goods or services being valued.

Cluster sampling is a two-stage random sampling used when there are meaningful subgroups within the population. In the first stage a random set of clusters are chosen. The second stage involves selecting respondents randomly from the chosen clusters. A variant is to choose all subjects or respondents within the chosen cluster.

Cognitive interview is a face-to-face method wherein a respondent's thoughts regarding questions and options in an interview are gathered.

Computer-aided personal interview is a face-to-face (or personal) interview in which the respondent or interviewer records responses in an electronic device.

Consequentiality is the respondent's belief that the hypothetical scenario is real, that his response will influence the decisions to implement the program, and that he will be asked to pay should the program be implemented.

Contingent valuation method is a stated preference approach that relies on directly asking or eliciting people's value for nonmarketed benefits through a survey.

Contingent valuation scenario is the most important part of a CV questionnaire. It typically includes a description of three important elements: (i) the program or policy/change of interest, (ii) the constructed market, and (iii) the method of payment.

Damage cost avoided is a direct proxy valuation method wherein the value of a policy or project is deduced from the damage costs that could have been incurred in the absence of the policy or project.

Dichotomous choice format is a general classification of CV elicitation formats, wherein respondents are allowed to respond only with yes or no answers to the CV question (i.e., binary choice responses).

Direct proxy method is a nonmarket valuation approach used when a marketed good or service can proxy for a nonmarketed one.

Direct use values are benefits associated with the consumption of a good or service.

Double-bounded dichotomous choice model is a variant of the single-bounded dichotomous choice model in which respondents are asked whether or not they are willing to pay an initial bid price. Based on their answer to this initial willingness-to-pay question, a follow-up bid price is offered, and they are asked again whether they are willing to pay for this follow-up bid.

Enumerator bias refers to enumerator-specific results as a consequence of an enumerator's willful and/or unconscious deviation from the agreed survey administration protocols.

Enumerator is the person who conducts the CVM survey in the field.

Existence value is a value assigned to goods and services simply because they exist.

Face-to-face survey is a survey that is administered in person.

Focus group discussion is a method of gathering information on a particular issue or topic by gathering a group of people from similar backgrounds or experiences.

Hedonic pricing estimates the value of nonmarketed goods and services by linking them to property or labor markets. It uses either spatial or temporal variation in the prices of real estate properties to deduce the value of environmental amenities.

Hypothetical bias is the difference between hypothetical and actual statements of value.

Incentive compatibility is the provision of adequate incentives for the respondent to reveal truthfully his value for the good or services.

Indirect use value is the benefit derived usually from ecosystem goods and services that are indirectly used by an agent. These are often associated with regulating services from ecosystems.

Information bias stems from observation that the type and quality of the information provided to respondents about a public or private good can strongly influence their willingness to pay especially under conditions of high personal relevance.

Interview fatigue or respondent fatigue occurs when respondents become tired during the interview because of the length or difficulty in answering the survey questions. This eventually leads to a deterioration in the quality of the survey responses.

Likert scale is a five-to-seven-point scale used to measure the degree of a respondent's agreement to a statement.

Logit regression model is a regression model that uses the logistic function to examine the relationship between a binary dependent variable and a set of covariates.

Mandatory payments are compulsory payment vehicles such as taxes or fees that all CV survey respondents face.

Multiple-bound discrete choice is a hybrid model in which respondents are presented with a range of bids similar to the payment card model. However, for each bid the respondent is asked to state the degree by which they think they are willing to pay (i.e., whether they are definitely not willing to pay, probably not willing to pay, not sure of willingness to pay, probably willing to pay, or definitely willing to pay).

Nonexcludability means that the good can be accessed and used by all people.

Nonmarket valuation is a set of methods used to measure people's willingness to pay for certain goods and services that are not traded in a market.

Nonrepresentative samples are samples that are not representative of the characteristics of the population from which they are drawn.

Nonrivalrous means that the goods do not dwindle in supply as more people consume them.

Oath script is a statement in the CV questionnaire that makes the respondent take an oath that he or she is declaring his or her true value for the hypothetical good or service.

Option value is a service or good that may have value not due to current use, but rather for their potential and future use.

Payment card is an elicitation format in which respondents are asked to choose their maximum willingness to pay from a range of possible bid prices.

Payment vehicle refers to the mechanism used to collect money from households or tourists to finance the hypothetical provision of the good. The "payment vehicle" could either be voluntary or mandatory.

Payment vehicle bias provides the context for the payment vehicle (e.g., tax, utility bills, voluntary contributions) that could affect the stated willingness to pay.

Pen-and-paper personal interviews protocol involves field data that are manually encoded in a pen-and-paper personal interview.

Principal component analysis is a method that reduces the dimensions of large data sets by converting them to a smaller set that still contains the information of the original set.

Probability sampling is a sampling method that gives the members of the sampling frame an equal chance of being chosen, by taking at random a specified number of samples from the list.

Probit regression model is a regression model that uses the inverse standard normal distribution function to examine the relationship between a binary dependent variable and a set of covariates.

Productivity change method is used when the nonmarketed good or service can be considered as an input in the production of a marketed good. The value of the nonmarketed good or service is deduced from changes in the value of the output of the marketed good.

Protest correction is a method to correct potential response biases by identifying and removing respondents whose "no" answer in the hypothetical referendum vote can be classified as protest votes.

Provision point mechanism is a condition or rule that triggers the provision of the promised change in the hypothetical scenario.

Referendum is an event in which the people vote for or against a specific issue.

Revealed preference approach is a suite of valuation methodologies that relies on observing actual choices and behavior in a related market.

Sampling frame is a list of all elements or respondents in a target population from which a sample can be drawn.

Scope insensitivity occurs when the willingness to pay of respondents are not sensitive to the quantity or size of the good or services.

Single-bounded dichotomous choice model is an elicitation format that asks respondents whether or not they are willing to pay a certain fixed amount (technically called a bid price) to receive a hypothetical change in the provision of a good or service.

Starting point bias is the observed tendency of respondents to rely or base their willingness to pay or value for the good or service on the initial bid that is offered. It is also sometimes referred to as the anchoring effect.

Stratified random sampling is a random sampling method that begins by dividing the entire sampling frame into a mutually exclusive stratum. The strata can be geographic or based on specific characteristics of the population, for example, between rural and urban areas, foreign and local tourists, or based on income categories in the population.

Substitute cost is a direct proxy valuation method in which the value of nonmarketed goods and services are equated with the cost of marketed goods and services providing same level of benefits as substitute.

Systematic sampling is a sampling method in which respondents or households are drawn in a deterministic way or decided based on a theoretical criterion. For instance, by using a deterministic rule of interviewing every fifth house in a block.

Total economic value presents the net sum of all the relevant willingness-to-pay and willingness-to-accept values associated with the changes or impacts brought about by a policy or project.

Transaction technical assistance is linked to an ADB-financed project or program. It prepares and enhances the implementation readiness of a specific ensuing project, develops capacity, and provides policy advice.

Travel cost method is a nonmarket valuation technique that has been developed to capture recreational value. It relies on the observation that travel and recreation are weak complements, and that travel and access costs are behaviorally equivalent.

Time-to-think protocol involves splitting the interview into two sessions. In the first session, the enumerator completes part of the questionnaire and introduces the CV scenario and questions to the respondent but does not ask for the answers. The response to the CV question is recorded in the second session, thereby giving the respondent time to contemplate or think about the CV scenario overnight.

Willingness to pay is a way to measure or deduce how people value goods and services through the trade-offs they are willing to make.

Yea-saying behavior is the tendency of respondents to overly agree to an offered bid either because they find the hypothetical scenario to be difficult to comprehend or feel that the scenario is inconsequential to them.

Appendix 1: Composition of a CV Study Team and Roles

Expertise	Role in the CV Study
Economist[a]	Should have in-depth knowledge and field experience on contingent valuation (CV) studies. Provides overall guidance and leads the development of the CV study design framework; survey implementation plan; CV data management and analysis. Interprets CV data results for conducting the project economic analysis; and prepares a draft of the final CV study report. The CV expert reports directly to the project lead, liaises with other project technical team members and other relevant government agencies, and provides overall direction for the CV survey team.
Technical team (e.g., financial specialist, project engineers, safeguard specialists, and others)[b]	The technical team comprises usually other specialists or experts engaged in the overall project implementation or preparation, who can be a good source of technical information, particularly on project design and scope, as well as related policy strategies or project-related programs.
The survey team[c] • Local field researcher supervisor • Local field coordinator/s • Local enumerators • Data analyst/manager/ local statistician	The survey team can be from a reputable local survey firm or national research agency with expertise on survey implementation and data processing. The survey team works closely with the economists on developing the CV design framework (sampling and survey development), facilitates focus group discussions and key informant interviews, and carries out the survey and implementation (pretest and deployment); selects and trains field enumerators; and monitors and conducts quality checks of survey instruments and manages, encodes, and processes the survey data.
Local collaborators (e.g., local partner agencies, nongovernment organizations [NGOs], the private sector, etc.)	Serve as key respondents for the key informant interviews. They are usually local officials from partner agencies, health workers, NGOs, or the private sector who can be a credible source of useful information, data, etc. useful for the CV study.

[a] The mission leader should look for an economist with a postgraduate degree who has in-depth knowledge and field experience on CV design to undertake the CV study.

[b] The technical team can already be part of the overall project team engaged in the transaction technical assistance. Collaboration in terms of specific inputs or to validate technical aspects of the projects may be required to support building the CV design.

[c] Generally, it is beneficial to team up with local academic institutions for CV surveys. In addition to having a large cadre of committed students who can serve as enumerators, these institutions generate goodwill with the local population and provide access to email, library resources, and a community of field-based researchers.

Source: Authors.

Appendix 2: Choice Experiment as an Alternative to Contingent Valuation

Introduction

Choice modeling (CM) or choice experiment (CE) is a type of stated preference valuation method. Like contingent valuation method (CVM), it is a survey-based approach to elicit a sample's willingness to pay (WTP) for nonmarketed goods and services used and produced by a program or project. However, unlike CVM, CM is an attribute-based stated choice method. The choice task of respondents in a CM involves choosing among different descriptions of the goods or services being valued. These descriptions are constructed by varying the attribute levels of these goods and services. The advantages of CM over other stated and revealed preference approaches are (Hanley et al. 2001; WHO 2012 ; Koeml and Yu 2020) as follows:

i) Makes respondents think about trade-offs and examine their true preferences.

ii) Permits valuation of both the good and services as well as its individual attributes and is therefore highly appropriate when changes are multidimensional or multi-attribute.

iii) Provides more information than discrete choice CV studies because the same respondent repeatedly chooses over different payment amounts and characterization of a good or service attributes. Repeated observation also allows for smaller sample sizes.

iv) It can provide information on the strength of preferences and trade-offs respondents are willing to make, and the probability of take-up or payment.

However, as a valuation method, there are disadvantages associated with CM, as Hanley et al. (2001) have identified:

i) The main disadvantage is that it is cognitively difficult because experimental designs may contain multiple complex choices between bundles with many attributes and levels.

ii) To estimate the total value of a program or good from CE, as distinct from a change in one of its attributes, CE studies assume that the value of the whole is equal to the sum of the parts. However, this assumption is problematic because there may be additional attributes of the good that are not included in the design and that the value of the "whole" may not be additive.

iii) Welfare estimates obtained with CE are sensitive to study design.

iv) To date, there is no clear evidence that CE is free from the common problems encountered with CVM, particularly in relation to consequentiality and truthful revelation of preferences and value.

CM has been compared with CV studies. The comparison results have been mixed, and there is no overwhelming evidence that one is favored over the other. In a review of studies that have compared CE and CV, Lloyd-Smith, Zawojska, and Adamiwicz (2018) note that these studies have not compared value estimates from equivalent surveys or in comparable econometric analyses. Failing to control design differences could significantly affect the differences between the estimated WTP values from these methods. Johnston et al. (2017) cite three primary considerations when selecting between the two techniques: First, is the marginal WTP for attributes or total WTP that is the value of interest? Second, a more field-oriented reason: are respondents viewing the evaluated good based on its individual attributes or as a whole? Finally, how could the framing of the valuation task affect the respondents' understanding of the good?

Designing Choice Experiments

Choice modeling, being a stated preference approach, shares common activities with a contingent valuation study. These commonalities include pre-survey activities such as identifying goods and services to be valued, initial qualitative research such as focus group discussions (FGDs) and key informant interviews (KIIs) to contextualize the hypothetical market and institutional scenario, and survey implementation design decisions related to survey sampling design and format. However, some specific activities or steps are specific to CM. These activities are (i) identifying the attributes and attribute levels, and (ii) experimental design and questionnaire development. Experimental design is not part of CVM, since CV studies have fixed attributes and levels. We discuss these steps in turn:

Identifying Attributes and Attribute Levels

The first step in designing a choice experiment is to identify the relevant attributes that define the benefits or goods and services produced by development programs and projects. This step is essential and fundamental because the subsequent design of the choice experiment rests on this activity.

Selecting attributes can begin with a review of literature on previous related studies. However, qualitative research through FGDs and KIIs is essential and indispensable. Attributes that are policy relevant and those that would likely affect people's choices or preferences should be chosen. Qualitative groundwork ensures that selected attributes are those to which respondents will probably respond and those that are likely to affect their choice. The FGD also helps gauge people's understanding of the attributes. Consultations with experts also help identify policy-relevant attributes, foremost of which are those related to bids or prices.

It is prudent to identify all likely relevant variables that are choice and policy relevant. However, not all should be included in the final experimental design. Again, FGDs and KIIs conducted with all affected stakeholders would help narrow down the number of attributes. Although no specific rule prescribes the number of attributes to consider, it has been common to use five to eight attributes in choice modeling studies. The number of attributes affects the complexity of the experimental design and can increase the respondents' cognitive burden. The complexity of choice tasks would ultimately affect the results. The price or bid, however, is a mandatory attribute. The trade-offs respondents are willing to make between the bid or price and the other attributes lead to identifying the willingness to pay for specific attributes of the good or service.

Once identified, the attributes need to be described in levels, which are the qualitative (i.e., categorical) or quantitative (i.e., numerical) descriptions of the attributes. For example, Table A2.1 shows some possible attribute levels for a project that improves water quality. Attributes such as the bid or price are often assigned continuous levels. On the other hand, attributes such as water quality and pressure can be assigned categorical levels representing descriptive variations in them. There are also no rules in assigning the type of levels for each attribute. What is essential is that the levels are clear and help differentiate varying characteristics of each attribute from the perspective of respondents. Hence, pilot or pretesting of questionnaires as well as the pre-survey FGDs and KIIs are essential for choice experiment or modeling studies.

Table A2.1: Attributes and Levels of a Water Quality Improvement Project

Attribute	Level 1		Level 2		Level 3	
Water availability	6 hours a day		12 hours a day		24 hours a day	
Water quality	Water looks good but does not smell and taste good		Water looks and smells good but does not taste good		Water looks, smells, and tastes good	
Water pressure	Weak		Medium		Strong	
Surcharge (price/ bid)/cubic meter	Level 1 ₱10	Level 2 ₱20	Level 3 ₱30	Level 4 ₱40	Level 5 ₱50	Level 6 ₱60

Source: Authors.

Experimental Design

Designing the experiment consists of the following activities:

Creating alternatives. The attributes and levels can be combined to form an alternative. An alternative is a specific description of the good or service that is being valued. Continuing with the example of a water quality improvement project, two possible alternatives from the attributes and levels presented in Table A2.1 are shown in Table A2.2. From this example, a total of 162 alternatives (three attributes with three levels and one attribute with six levels, i.e., $3^3 \times 6^1 = 162$) can be formed. If the status quo levels of the attributes are not included, an additional alternative can be constructed. This status quo alternative is also called the opt-out alternative, and it describes the pre-project levels of attributes.

Table A2.2: Two Possible Alternatives Constructed from Attributes and Levels

Attribute	Alternative 1	Alternative 2
Water availability	6 hours a day	24 hours a day
Water quality	Water looks good but does not smell and taste good	Water looks good and smells good but does not taste good
Water pressure	Medium	Weak
Surcharge (price/bid)/ cubic meter	₱10	₱40

Source: Authors.

Creating choice sets. The alternatives are combined to form a choice set. The task of the respondent is to choose between at least two alternatives in a choice set.

Choice Modeling as a Potential Solution to Some Issues in Economic Analysis of Projects

The economic analyses of projects in which a stated preference approach was used to benefit valuation have been often based on CVM. CM can, however, potentially be a solution to some of the issues associated with the use of CVM for economic analysis of projects.

One of the issues that have affected the implementation of CVM is the timing of various project preparatory activities. There may be instances where the technical studies, which include the engineering designs and feasibility studies, are not yet available at the time the economic analysis is conducted, causing uncertainty in the level of goods or services projects can deliver. The rigidity of CVM scenario designs may not be robust to uncertainty in project designs. The WTP estimate from CVM is specific to a fixed attribute level of the good embodied in the CV scenario. If actual or final project design and benefits deviate from those used in the CV scenario, the WTP estimates may not reflect the true value of respondents for the project. On the other hand, since CM analysis produces different WTP estimates for different attribute levels, it is more flexible in the face of uncertain project design and benefits—because it can match an appropriate WTP estimate for a different project or benefit scales.

Aside from being more flexible amid uncertainty in project benefit levels, CM can also provide ex-ante information for project design, particularly in its scale and components, made possible because of the variation in the levels of the attributes. Estimates of the WTP can therefore be obtained for individual attributes and specific levels of an attribute. These estimates give more information on people's preferences for project design components and scale even before the availability of engineering designs and feasibility studies.

Another issue with the application of CVM in project economic analysis is the use of multiple WTP questions. Multiple WTP questions occur when several projects lead to different benefits but have a common payment vehicle. This situation is common for water supply and sanitation projects that have water quality improvement and sewerage improvement components. Hypothetical payments for these improvements are often collected through new water bills or surcharges.

A series of WTP questions can be prone to respondent confusion and ordering effects in the presence of budget constraints. A well-designed choice experiment can avoid these issues. It can be argued that the CM format is no different because it also asks for a series of choice tasks. There is a significant difference, however, between CM and CVM in this aspect. In a CM study, choice sets are presented to respondents independent of each other. This presentation allows a "reset" between choice sets, and thus, it is as if the respondent is facing the same or constant budget constraint for every choice set. In the CVM format, there is no "reset," giving respondents a feeling that the hypothetical expenses add up across the series of WTP questions.

Appendix 3: Benefit Transfer Methods

Using the Benefit Transfer Method to Estimate Project Benefits

Many ADB projects face time and resource constraints. In estimating project benefits, the benefit transfer method is often used in lieu of conducting a primary valuation study. The benefit transfer method uses previously established unit values of benefits that were estimated for study sites with similar characteristics as the proposed project site. Caution is needed when applying this approach, as many benefits are site specific, and are not appropriate to transfer. When a transfer is performed, a suitable adjustment is needed for all important differences—from one type of goods and services and beneficiary populations and context to another—between the original study site and the area for which estimates are being projected..

The two main methods of benefit transfer are the unit value transfer and value function transfer. The unit value transfer uses either a single value or an aggregation or average of values from a previously valued study site to estimate the value of proposed services in the project site. Values can be adjusted to reflect differences between the study and project sites (e.g., income and price levels). The value function transfer uses a valuation function estimated for a study site, calibrated according to the characteristics of the project site.

Brander (2015) summarizes the general steps of the value transfer method as follows:

1. **Describe the baseline, with-project scenario, and target beneficiaries.** Provide information on the baseline level of provision of services in the absence of the project vis-a-vis the extent of change in services with the project. If the change in provision of services is expected to happen gradually, the temporal profiles of the change should be described as well. Accurately identify the target beneficiaries

to be able to correctly adjust values for population characteristics and compute aggregate values to estimate the value of the service provided by the project.

2. **Select relevant study site data.** Gather existing valuation studies conducted for study sites similar to the project site in terms of services to be provided, baseline level provision, with-project level provision, and characteristics of beneficiaries. Choose previous studies of good quality in terms of valuation methods used, application of method, data used (sampling procedure, representativeness, and sample size), and statistical significance of value estimates or function.

3. **Transfer values**

   a. Determine whether the values are to be transferred in terms of beneficiaries (e.g., $ per household) or ecosystem (e.g., $ per hectare). The contingent valuation method produces estimates of willingness to pay per beneficiary, whereas others produce estimates of values per physical or areal unit.

   b. Select the value transfer method. The method to use will depend on the availability of study site value data and the similarity of the study and the project sites. In general, unit value transfer is used when study and policy sites are very similar; and value function transfer is used if there are significant differences between the study and project sites.

   c. Estimate unit value at the project site. When unit transfer value is deemed appropriate, obtain the value per unit or average unit value from study site valuation results. Make the necessary adjustments for differences between the study and policy sites. Quantify the change in service provision in the project site and multiply the unit value by the change units at the policy site to estimate the aggregate change in service value.

      When using value function transfer, select an estimated value function that relates to the services to be provided by the proposed project and the characteristics of the beneficiaries. A value function is a regression equation in which the dependent variable is the value of the service (e.g., willingness to pay for a service) and the independent variables include characteristics of the service and the beneficiaries. The estimation of the value of services in the project site is illustrated in Box A3.1.

Box A3.1: Sample Application of Benefit Transfer Methods

Example 1: Unit Value Transfer

The proposed project will improve the clarity of coastal waters. A choice experiment valuation study on water clarity has been conducted recently for a study site similar to the project site. The study site unit value yields willingness to pay per household per year of $20.51 at 2010 price levels for an improvement from "medium" to "high" water clarity. Multiplying $20.51 by the number of households at the project site (19,938) gives an aggregate estimate of the welfare improvement for an improvement in water clarity from "medium" to "high" of $408,928 per year. Note that if the original estimate is for 2010 and the project benefits are expressed in 2021 base year, the unit value of service estimated from the study site valuation should be adjusted using the appropriate price index (as illustrated in the box table).

Example 2: Value Function Transfer

The proposed project will improve the quality of water in a river. A contingent valuation study was conducted in a study site which is significantly different from the project site in terms of income level, location, and characteristics of beneficiaries. The box table below illustrates how to calculate willingness to pay for the proposed service provided by the project using the benefit transfer method. From the probit model of the primary valuation study, the estimated coefficients are multiplied by the means of the independent variables for the project site. The sum of the products of the coefficients and the means plus the constant (8.10) is then divided by the absolute value of the bid coefficient (0.19) derived for the study site. The calculation yields willingness to pay of $42.62 per household per month for the service provided by the proposed project.

Benefit Function Transfer Calculation

Variables	Value Function Coefficients (A)	Mean, Project Site Characteristics (B)	(A)*(B)
Bid price	-0.19		
Household income	0.0003	21,302	6.3906
Age of head	0.004	44.21	0.17684
Gender	0.003	0.49	0.00147
Distance from river	-0.003	2.52	-0.00756
Pollution level	0.04	8.4	0.336
Constant	1.2		1.2
Total			8.09735
Willingness to pay = (8.09735/0.19) = 42.61763			

Sources: Brander (2015); ADB (2017).

d. Assess uncertainties through value ranges, distribution of values, confidence interval, sensitivity analysis, and calculation of transfer errors.

4. **Report results.** Describe all key judgments and assumptions, and report value estimates along with clear information about the uncertainty of the estimates.

Although a straightforward method, benefit transfer requires careful application. The main challenge is to ensure reliability of generated estimates, given the inherent errors associated with it. Boutwell and Westra (2013) categorize errors associated with benefit transfer into measurement errors and transfer errors. Measurement errors are errors "related to the primary valuation study from which value is to be transferred. It is associated with the assumptions made and methodology employed in the primary study and the resulting divergence between the actual value of a service in question and the estimate of that value generated by the primary study." Newbold et al. (2018) emphasizes that it is necessary to verify the internal validity of value estimates reported in existing nonmarket valuation studies before using them for benefit transfer. The primary valuation study must use a reliable nonmarket valuation method and experimental design that is free of systematic biases. Another concern is selection bias, which is related to the choice of primary valuation study. The bias may come from choosing only studies that meet narrow criteria related to the research question or studies that have been widely published, thereby excluding other useful literature.

Transfer errors are associated with the process of transferring the benefit value. These errors are related to "dissimilarities between the study site and the policy site, the method used to transfer values, or from a lack of consistency with respect to the economic construct under investigation" (Boutwell and Westra 2013). The next discussion will focus on the first source of error: dissimilarities between the study and project sites.

In many cases, the study and project sites have important differences in characteristics which when disregarded may result to under- or overestimation of project benefits. Table A3.1 below summarizes these common characteristics and how adjustments should be made to account for their differences.

Table A3.1: Adjusting for Common Differences between Study and Project Sites

Characteristic	Adjustment	Formula for Adjustment	Illustration
Differences in income	Use income elasticity of willingness to pay for the service in question. Elasticity values are available from primary valuation studies and meta-analyses that include income as an explanatory variable.	$WTP_p = WTP_s\ (Yp/Ys)^E$ where: WTPp = willingness to pay at the policy site WTPs = willingness to pay at the study site Yp = income per capita at the policy site Ys = income per capita at the study site *E* = income elasticity of willingness to pay	WTPs = $20.51 Yp = $48,750 Ys = $36,240 *E* = 0.43 Following the formula: WTP_p = US$ 18.05 = 20.51 x (36,240 / 48,750)$^{0.43}$
Value estimate in the primary valuation study expressed in price level of previous years	Adjust values to account for inflation, using available price indices or GDP deflators.	$WTP_p = WTP_s\ (Dp/Ds)$ where: WTP_P = willingness to pay at the policy site WTP_S = willingness to pay at the study site D_P = GDP deflator index for the year of the policy site assessment D_S = GDP deflator index for the year of the study site valuation	WTP_S = $20.51 D_P = 116 D_S = 111 WTP_P = $21.44 = 20.51 x (116 / 111)
Benefit value estimated by a primary valuation study conducted in a different country	Adjust to account for differences in purchasing power and currency using purchasing power parity adjusted exchange rate	$WTP_p = WTP_s * E$ where: WTP_P = willingness to pay in currency of the policy site WTP_S = willingness to pay in the currency of the study site E = purchasing power parity adjusted exchange rate between policy and study site currencies (can be obtained from the World Bank's World Development Indicators)	WTP_S = $20.15 E = 2.07 WTP_P = 42.46 in local currency= $20.51*2.07

Source: Brander (2015).

Appendix 4: A Sample CV Scenario for Improvement in Water Supply

This project assessed Metro Manila residents' willingness to pay for the protection and conservation of the four main watershed areas that provide the main water source of Metro Manila. The project also investigated how "water user's fee" can be used to design the best policy mechanism for water supply management.[1]

Presentation of the Water Supply Situation

Metropolitan Manila, with a population of more than 11 million, has been experiencing water supply problems for its residents and industries. The problem is especially serious during the dry season, when water rationing is common in many areas. Rapid population growth, increasing incomes, the rise of industries, people migrating to the city, and urbanization have all contributed to the escalating demand for water. Unfortunately, the quantity and quality of water available for these uses have not kept up with this growing demand.

Metro Manila's domestic water supply comes from the Angat, Ipo, Umiray, and La Mesa watersheds. The National Power Corporation has jurisdiction over the Angat, the Department of Environment and Natural Resources over Ipo and Umiray watersheds, while the ABS-CBN Foundation, through its Bantay Kalikasan program, has been given the task of managing the La Mesa watershed.

[The interviewer will show photographs of the four watersheds and describe the conditions of each.]

The Manila Water and Sewerage System, a government agency, used to be responsible for water distribution in Metro Manila. Recently, distribution has been privatized and is now being handled by the Manila Water Company (for the east zone) and the Maynilad Water Services (for the west zone).

---

1 Calderon et al. (2005).

[The interviewer will show and discuss newspaper headlines about the water supply problems of Metro Manila in recent years.]

Perhaps you are aware that water tariffs have recently increased. You may also have heard about the problems the water distributors have encountered, for example, that one of them is losing money.

Description of the Role of Forests and Watersheds in Sustainable Water Supply

[The interviewer will describe the role of forests and watersheds in sustainable water supply and show pictures of degraded and well-managed watersheds.]

[The interviewer demonstrates this by using a plastic bottle cut into half with the smaller hole as the outlet, a container of water, and a piece of towel large enough to cover the hole of the plastic bottle. Initially, the interviewer pours only a small amount, which the towel will absorb. As more water is added, some of it will drain or be retained on the surface, representing a "flood."]

A watershed is like a kitchen sink. You've seen how the kitchen sink catches water from the faucet and drains it into an outlet. The watershed works in a similar manner. It also catches water, though from the rain and not from the faucet, and drains the water through a network of rivers and streams in the area, until it reaches a common outlet.

You can also think of the soil in the watershed as a sponge that absorbs water. If you cover the sink with a sponge and turn on the faucet, it will take some time before water is drained because the sponge will absorb most of it first. Thus, the more water is absorbed, the less goes down the drain. In the case of watersheds, the more water they absorb, the less water goes to the lowlands. In effect, the more water is absorbed, the lesser floods will occur. Also, the more water is stored in the watershed, the better water supply will be during times when there is no rain. We are not saying, however, that a well-managed watershed will prevent the occurrence of floods and droughts. With prolonged rains, floods can result even with the best-managed watersheds. Likewise, droughts can happen during extremely long dry seasons.

However, the amount of water that can be stored in the watershed is largely affected by its land uses. It is widely accepted that maintaining a good forest cover increases the capacity of the watershed to store water and regulate its flow. But as you may already know, our country is fast losing its forest cover. Deforestation and poor land use practices are common, and these have damaged the hydrologic condition of many of our watersheds. Therefore, floods during the rainy season and droughts during the dry season are common.

The Trust Fund

At present, the money paid by water users to the water distributors is mainly for treating and distributing water to the users. Very little, if any, is used for watershed management. The agencies responsible for managing and protecting the watersheds lack the financial resources necessary to effectively carry out their tasks. If these agencies have additional funds, they can

- reforest a bigger area in the watershed per year;
- hire more forest guards to protect the watershed;
- construct more lookout towers;
- install more soil erosion control structures (vegetative and engineering);
- acquire communication and transportation facilities for better patrolling and protection of the watershed;
- conduct other activities to enhance people's awareness about the benefits derived from the watersheds; and
- involve various stakeholders in watershed management and protection activities.

The CV Question

Studies like this one have been conducted to estimate people's willingness to pay for the improvement of an environmental good. The respondents were presented with hypothetical situations, and the payments were also hypothetical, as they will be for you. (In other words, the new situation described did not actually exist yet, and the respondents did not have to pay for anything on the spot). The results of these studies show that some people tend not to reveal their true willingness to pay. Or they simply choose not to cooperate.

Why would a respondent not reveal his or her willingness to pay or refuse to cooperate? I guess the most obvious answer is that the respondents are afraid that they might be made to pay.

But I would like to request you to think carefully about whether you really care for reliable water supply or not. Also, remember that this study was not commissioned by the water distributors but came about because of the research team's desire to find out how water users feel about protecting the basic resource that produces water. There are no right or wrong answers to the questions I will pose.

Suppose a trust fund for the improved management of the four watersheds will be created. The trust fund will be managed by a council composed of various stakeholders—water users like you, water distributors (Maynilad and Manila Water), the government (Department of Environment and Natural Resources/National Water Resources Board, Manila Water and Sewerage System), Local Water Utilities Administration, local government units, nongovernment organizations, and academia. This council will decide on the activities that will be supported by the fund, all of which should directly be related to watershed management. Under no circumstance will the fund be used for any other purpose.

Before the establishment of this trust fund, the government will consult the water users through a referendum. The result of the referendum will determine whether the trust fund for the management of the watershed will be established or not.

(NOTE TO THE ENUMERATOR: Before proceeding to the next question, make sure the respondent fully understood the concept of the trust fund.)

If you will participate in a referendum, will you vote for a legislation that will create the trust fund if its passage requires all water users to contribute P____ / household/month to this trust fund through their water bill?

Appendix 5: A Sample Illustration of a Full CV Survey Questionnaire for a Water Services Improvement Project

MODULE 1: Background and Purpose of Study

To improve water supply services provided by the ABC Water Authority, the local government of City A will fund the **ABC Urban Water Services Improvement Project (AUWSIP)** with the assistance of the national government and the Asian Development Bank. AUWSIP will support the rehabilitation of existing outdated water treatment plants, water pumping stations, replacement of 700 kilometers (km) of damaged pipes, and replacement of 146,000 high quality and reliable water meters to improve the water distribution system and management, which will result in reduction of nonrevenue water (NRW) to 20% or less, increase water supply from 100 liters per capita per day (lpcd) to 135 lpcd and supply period from 6–10 hours to 24 hours in a day.

This survey aims to solicit opinions and suggestions from respondents in the project area to help improve the project design to maximize the benefits of the project to consumers.

We would like to request that only household heads (husband or wife or whoever makes household decisions) should answer the questionnaire. Please be assured that any information you provide will remain confidential and will not be used for any purpose other than as mentioned above. You have the right not to participate in this survey. However, should you choose to participate, please remember that there is no right or wrong answer. We would only like you to give us your honest opinion. It will probably take you about 30–45 minutes to complete the questionnaire. Thank you.

SCREENER

S1.	Are you willing to take part in this survey?	1. Yes 2. No	Continue Ask S2 and TERMINATE
S2.	If no, please indicate reason.		
S3.	Are you connected to the ABC Water Authority (AWA)?	Yes No	Check QUOTA for household with/without piped connection

A. General Information

A.1	Date of interview	
A.2	Name of enumerator	
A.3.	Locality	
A.4.	Name of respondent	
A.5	Phone no. (optional)	
A.6	Address of respondent	
A.7	Respondent category	1. Head of household 2. Spouse of head of household 3. Child of household head 4. Other, please specify ________________

MODULE 2: Current Good/Service Conditions, Consumption Patterns, and Use Behavior

B. Water Sources and Uses

B.1	What is the main source of water of your household?	1. Piped water (into house) 2. Piped water (into yard/plot) 3. Public tap/standpipe 4. Tube well/borehole 5. Dug well 6. Spring 7. Rainwater 8. Tanker truck 9. Cart with small tank 10. Surface water (river/dam/lake/pond/ stream/canal/irrigation channel) 11. Bottled water 12. Community RO (reverse osmosis) plant 13. Others, please specify

NOTE:
If source is 1 or 2, go to Section C.
If source is 3 through 13, go to Section D.

C. For Households with Piped Connections

C.1	Is your connection metered?	1. Yes, meter working. 2. Yes, but meter not working. 3. No
C.2	What is your water consumption per month? (Last monthly bill)	____________ m^3 ____________
C.3	How many hours per day do you receive water from piped system?	________hours
C.4	How many days per week do you receive water from piped system?	________days
C.5	Adequacy of quantity of water	1. Adequate 2. Sometimes inadequate 3. Always inadequate
C.6	How is the pressure of supply?	1. Very good 2. Good 3. Satisfactory 4. Not satisfactory 5. Bad

C.7	How do you describe the quality of your piped water supply?	1. Very good 2. Good 3. Satisfactory 4. Not satisfactory 5. Bad 6. Very bad
C.7a	Taste of water	1. Very good 2. Good 3. Satisfactory 4. Not satisfactory 5. Bad 6. Very bad
C.7b	Color of water	1. Colorless 2. Yellow/turbid, sometimes 3. Yellow/turbid, frequently
C.7c	Smell of water	1. Odorless 2. Bad odor, sometimes 3. Bad odor, always
C.8	Is there any relation between the quality of water and illness in your household?	1. Yes 2. No
C.9	How many persons in your household were ill during the past year due to consumption of unsafe water?	________________Adult ________________Children
C.9a	How many days of work were lost due to these illnesses?	Average days in the past year ________
C.9b	How many days of school were lost due to these illnesses?	Average days in the past year ________
C.9c	If the sick person got treatment, how much was the medical cost?	Consultation ____________ Medicine ____________ (Pharmacy) Herbal Medicine ____________ Transportation ____________ Hospitalization ____________ Others, specify ____________ TOTAL ____________ (Interviewer to compute)
C.10	Do you treat water before drinking?	1. Yes 2. No (Go to C.14)
C.11	What do you usually do to water to make it safer to drink?	1. Boil 2. Add bleach/chlorine 3. Use water filters (without electricity) 4. Solar disinfection 5. Strain through a cloth 6. Let it stand and settle 7. Others, specify ___________

C.12	Do you incur cost when treating water?	1. Fuel cost 2. Electricity/power cost 3. Maintenance cost 4. Others, please specify ________
C.13	How much do you spend to treat water (in a month)?	____________________
C.14	How do you store water?	1. Bucket/vessel (covered) 2. Bucket/vessel (uncovered) 3. Drum 4. Tank (covered) 5. Tank (uncovered) 6. No storage 7. Others, please specify ________

C.15	Do you experience water service disruption?	1. Yes (Go to C.15a) 2. No (Go to C.16)
C.15a	How many hours or days before the service was restored?	________hours/days
C.15b	What is the frequency of disruption in a year?	________days
C16	Do you have any other water source aside from your in-house piped water?	1. Yes (Go to C.17) 2. No (Go to MODULE 3)

WATER FROM ALTERNATIVE SOURCES

C.17	C.17a	C.17b	C.17c	C.17d	C.17e	C.17f	C.17g
Please indicate other water sources used aside from piped during water disruption period (multiple response accepted).	Where is this water source located? (Write code)	How long does it take to go there, get water, and come back in one trip? (minutes/day)	How many times in a day do you or your household member collect water from this source?	Who usually goes to this water source to fetch water for the household? (write code)	How much is your average water consumption from this source per day? (specify how many liters/buckets/ gallon in a day)	Do you incur costs when you collect water from this source? (write code) 1. Yes 2. No	How much is your monthly cost for getting/using water from this source?[a]
1. Public tap/stand piped							
2. Tube well/borehole							
3. Dug well							
4. Spring							
5. Rain water							
6. Tanker trucks							
7. Cart with small tank							
8. Bottled water							
9. Surface water (river/ dam etc)							
10. Community RO plant							
11. Others, specify ______							

CODES:

C.17a. Location of Source
1. In own dwelling/house
2. In own yard
3. Elsewhere

C.17d. Water Collector
1. Adult lady
2. Girl child (under 15)
3. Adult male
4. Boy child (under 15)
5. All family members
6. Domestic help
7. Others, please specify

[a] Include operations and maintenance costs, payments made to delivery person or tanker service, cost of electricity, storage cost, cost of treatment, etc.

D. For Households without Piped Water Connection

D.1 Please indicate water sources used for the following activity and place: 1 for primary water source used, 2 for secondary, 3 for tertiary, etc. Also write down time spent collecting water, distance traveled, volume of consumption, and average monthly payment /expense per source.

Water Source	General Household Use (Multiple sources allowed)	Drinking or Cooking (Multiple sources allowed)	Time Spent Collecting Water from Source (minutes /day)	Distance Traveled to Collect Water from Source (km)	Who usually fetches water from source?[a] (Write code)	Average Consumption per Day (indicate if liters/buckets/ gallon)	How much is the monthly cost for getting/using water from this source?[b]
1. Public tap/stand piped							
2. Tube well/borehole							
3. Dug well							
4. Spring							
5. Rain water							
6. Tanker trucks							
7. Cart with small tank							
8. Bottled water							
9. Surface water (river/ dam, etc.)							
10. Community RO plant							
11. Others, specify ________							

CODES:
1. Adult lady
2. Girl child (under 15)
3. Adult male
4. Boy child (under 15)
5. All family members
6. Domestic help
7. Others, please specify

[b] Include operations and maintenance costs, payments made to delivery person or tanker service, cost of electricity, storage cost, etc.

D.2	How do you describe the quality of your primary source of water supply for drinking/cooking?	1. Very good 2. Good 3. Satisfactory 4. Not satisfactory 5. Bad 6. Very bad
D.2a	Taste of water	1. Very good 2. Good 3. Satisfactory 4. Not satisfactory 5. Bad 6. Very bad
D.2b	Color of water	1. Colorless 2. Yellow/turbid, sometimes 3. Yellow/turbid, frequently
D.2c	Smell of water	1. Odorless 2. Bad odor, sometimes 3. Bad odor, always
D.3	Is there any relation between the quality of water and illness in your household?	1. Yes 2. No
D.4	How many persons in your household were ill during the past year due to consumption of unsafe water?	________________ Adult ________________ Children
D.5a	How many days of work were lost due to these illnesses	Average days in the past year _____
D.5b	How many days of school were lost due to these illnesses	Average days in the past year _____
D.5c	If the sick person got treatment, how much was the medical cost?	Consultation __________ Medicine (Pharmacy) __________ Herbal medicine __________ Transportation __________ Hospitalization __________ Others, specify __________ TOTAL __________ (Interviewer to compute)
D.6	Do you treat water before drinking?	1. Yes 2. No (go to D.10)

D.7	What do you usually do to water to make it safer to drink?	1. Boil 2. Add bleach/chlorine 3. Use water filters (without electricity) 4. Solar disinfection 5. Strain through a cloth 6. Let it stand and settle 7. Others, specify ____________
D.8	Do you incur cost when treating water?	1. Fuel cost 2. Electricity/power cost 3. Maintenance cost 4. Others, please specify
D.9	How much do you spend to treat water (in a month)?	____________________________
D.10	How do you store water?	1. Bucket/vessel (covered) 2. Bucket/vessel (uncovered) 3. Drum 4. Tank (covered) 5. Tank (uncovered) 6. No storage 7. Others, please specify ________
D.11	How much is the cost of water storage? (Include installation/construction costs)	
D.12	Reasons for not having in-house water connection?	1. Connection fee too high 2. Monthly charges too high 3. Connection not available 4. Present arrangement satisfactory 5. Rented house 6. Waiting list 7. Others, please specify ________

MODULE 3: Contingent Valuation Scenario

Context and Problems

The ABC Water Authority (AWA) is mandated to develop and regulate water supply and wastewater in ABC City. In more recent years, water service provided by AWA has been deteriorating. Water supply has been intermittent, and low-pressure areas have developed due to lack of maintenance and rehabilitation of assets. The water distribution pipelines are suffering faults at a rate of 10 times the accepted norm, and approximately half of them need replacement. Nonrevenue water (NRW) has been steadily increasing and has reached 50% this year. The failing of the pipelines is placing an ever-increasing maintenance burden on AWA in keeping up with fixing leaks. As a result of the large NRW in the networks, all the water treatment plants servicing the city are challenged by the demand for higher volumes of water. Most water treatment plants are now operating above their respective design capacities and are using techniques and processes that fail to meet the drinking water quality standards of the local government. Consequently, the quality of water at customer taps has also deteriorated, increasing the risk to public health. Most water pump stations are operating above their respective design capacities, causing them to operate inefficiently and unreliably.

Description of the Water Quality Improvement Plan and Its Benefits

The proposed ABC Urban Water Services Improvement Project will support water supply improvement in ABC City by rebuilding resilient and sustainable infrastructure. Particularly, it will support the rehabilitation of existing outdated water treatment plants, water pumping stations, replacement of 700 kilometers (km) of damaged pipes, and replacement of 146,000 high-quality and reliable water meters to improve water distribution system and management, which will result in project outcomes listed in Table A5.1 below (hand over show card to respondent). Project interventions to improve the water supply system and its sustainable maintenance will require rationalization of water tariffs. AWA will utilize the tariff revenue only for the maintenance and upkeep of the system, through a ring-fenced accounting system.

Table A5.1: Without and With Project Scenarios

Attribute	Without Project	With Project
Water supply quantity	250 liters per household per day	500 liters per household per day
Water supply period	for 6–10 hours/day	for 24x7
Supply to vulnerable households	No proper supply	100%
Nonrevenue water (NRW)	51%	20%
Water Quality		
Taste	Tastes bad	Tastes sweet or good
Odor	Smells bad	No smell
Total Suspended Solids (TSS)	High level of TSS	Acceptable level of TSS (within standards)

Improving the water supply system and its delivery with above discussed activities will involve fund requirements. With the limited budget available the government will need to increase the tariff. In such case, the water supply development will make government and the consumers compromise other development or expenditure.

CV Question

Suppose that the ABC Water Authority decides to push through with the ABC Urban Water Services Improvement Project through a referendum. The project will only be implemented if 60% of households will vote for it. But with the implementation of the project, people would have to pay a higher water bill. If they vote against the plan, their water bills will not increase, but the water service and quality will not improve either.

This survey is only meant to get your opinion on whether you would decide to vote for the ABC Urban Water Services Improvement Project if it will be implemented in your area. Past studies show that people say YES when asked of their opinion in a survey, but they would vote NO in a real situation. Researchers are not sure why they do this. It could be because it feels good to say yes in a survey when you do not actually have to pay. Or it could be to please the person doing the interview. However, please try to tell us how you would answer in an actual situation. Please say yes only if you are really willing to support the plan to improve water quality services in your city.

Also please consider your household's capacity to pay. Payment for these improvements means forgoing other household expenditures.

Different households also have different water consumption and expenditures. The average household with five members consumes around 25 m^3 of water per month and pays ₱175/ month. You may not be one of the average households and may have a higher or lower consumption and bill than average. But I would like you to think as if you are an average household consuming and paying the average amount per month.

VERSION 1: FOR HOUSEHOLDS WITH PIPED WATER CONNECTION

E.1 Now, I want you to assume that the ABC Urban Water Services Improvement Project will provide your household 500 liters per day if it means that your household will have to pay an additional amount of ₱____/household/month to be added to your monthly water bill for improved water services?	Yes (go to E.5) No (go to E.6)

VERSION 2: FOR HOUSEHOLDS WITHOUT PIPED WATER CONNECTION

E.2 Now, I want you to assume that the ABC Urban Water Services Improvement Project will provide your household 500 liters per day if it means that your household will have to pay ₱____ /household/month per month as water charges?	Yes (go to E.3) No (go to E.6)
E.3 Do you prefer a fixed charge or metered bill?	Fixed charge Metered bill
E.4 If you want an in-house connection, how much are you willing to spend to have it installed (for connection fee, materials, and labor?	____________________

DEBRIEFING QUESTIONS

A. Reasons for Vote

E.5 Why did you agree to support the plan? (Choose one or more options, as applicable)	1. I am using the water services, therefore I should pay 2. I want to abide by the law 3. Quality and quantity of water will improve 4. Others, pls specify: ____________________

(Go to section B)

E.6 What is the main reason why you disagree to support the plan? (Choose one option)	1. I cannot afford the additional monthly fee 2. I am not sure about the sustainability of the plan 3. I don't like AWA managing the construction and operation of the project 4. I don't see the need for the project 5. I don't see need for rehabilitation of pipelines and water treatment 6. Others, pls specify: ___________________

(Go to section B)

B. Certainty Questions

E.7. How sure are you of your answer in E.1/E.2?	1. Very unsure 2. Unsure 3. Sure 4. Very sure

MODULE 4: Demographic and Socioeconomic Profile

F. Basic Household Information

F.1	Age of household (HH) Head	_________years
F.2	Gender of HH head	1. Male 2. Female
F.3	Civil status of HH head	1. Single 2. Married 3. Live- in 4. Divorced/Separated 5. Widowed
F.4	Occupation of HH head	1. Agriculture, fisheries, forestry 2. Service sector 3. Sales and office 4. Construction, extraction, and maintenance 5. Production, transportation, and material-moving 6. Management, professional, and related occupations
F.5	Education of HH head	1.Some elementary 2. Elementary graduate 3. Some high school 4. High school graduate 5. Some college 6. College graduate 7. Master's/PhD 8. Vocational

F.6	No. of persons living in the household	Children (12 yrs and below) ___________ Teen (13–17 yrs old) ___________ Adult (18 yrs and above) ___________ TOTAL ___________ (To be filled up by enumerator)
F.6a	No. of families in the household	
F.7	Estimated monthly household income *(Income of all household members who work, as well as income from other sources such as house rent, interest from savings account/ deposits, pension money and remittance money both local and abroad, excluding tax and social security premiums)*	₱_______/ mo
F.8	Estimated annual household income *(Income of all household members who work, as well as income from other sources such as house rent, interest from savings account/ deposits, pension money and remittance money both local and abroad, excluding tax and social security premiums)*	1. Less than 40,000 2. 40,000–59,999 3. 60,000–99,999 4. 100,000–250,000 5. Greater than 250,000
F.9	Estimated monthly HH expenditure	₱_______/ mo
F.9a	Estimated annual household expenditure	1. Less than 40,000 2. 40,000–59,000 3. 60,000–99,999 4. 100,000–250,000 5. Greater than 250,000
F.10	Year house was constructed?	_________
F.10a	Age of house	_________ years (To be filled up by enumerator based on answer to F.10)

F.11	Number of years family living in this house	_________years *(Note: this must be less than F.10)*
F.12	House ownership	1. Fully owned by respondent/family of respondent 2. Owned but still being amortized by respondent/family of respondent 3. Rented 4. Free use

Appendix 6: Conducting Field Interviews for CV Surveys

Good Practices in Survey Implementation

The following are some suggested field protocols when conducting CV surveys.

Proper Introduction by Enumerators

Enumerators must give a proper introduction of themselves, the purpose of the survey, the time required to complete it, the assurance of confidentiality for any shared information by the respondent, and more importantly, obtain consent from the respondent that he/she is willing to participate in the survey. If the respondent was randomly chosen from a sampling frame (i.e., list of households connected to the water district), the enumerator must also inform them of how their name was chosen. Enumerators should also be prepared to show survey credentials (ID, letter of endorsement from the mayor and local officials, etc.) should the respondent ask for it.

If a respondent declines to be interviewed, the enumerator will ask for the reason of his/her refusal. This will be recorded in a nonresponse monitoring sheet for future reporting.

Conducting Personal Interviews

Where to Do Interviews and Who to Interview

For an in-person interview, enumerators are cautioned not to conduct the interview by groups or in the presence of other people who are not part of the household (i.e., neighbors) as this may influence their response. Instead, the interview should be done in private and, if possible, at the home of the respondent. However, if the neighbor, for example, refuses to leave, the enumerator should explain to the respondent that he/she will return later for the interview.

It is also important to remind enumerators that they should interview only the head of the household or the person responsible for making decisions in the family.

How to Do the Interview

In a CV survey, respondents are often requested to undertake several different types of response tasks, which includes the following (Cummings, Brookshire, and Schulze 1986):

Recall: To solicit information on the actions or behavior pattern of the individual or household members over some period in the past (often in detail), i.e., over a year.

Partitioning: To assign a portion of time, number, or expenditures to engage in certain activities or meet certain objectives. Examples include a detailed report on the type of sanitation-related illnesses and the number of household members afflicted by such illness in the past year, by age and gender.

Assessment of a particular condition: To appraise a condition based on a described set of criteria, e.g., evaluation of current water supply in terms of quality, adequacy, timing, and pressure.

Truthful response on sensitive information: To report sensitive financial or personal information that may be factual but regarded by the individual as confidential such as income, expenditure, or assets.

Evaluation of attitudes: To evaluate the sentiments/opinion and attitudes/feelings of the respondent for a certain issue or condition, such as their belief in the success of the proposed program or their level of trust in the institutions mentioned in the CV scenario who will collect payment from households and manage the funds.

Projected responses to hypothetical circumstances: To describe actions under proposed conditions that have not occurred, e.g., what would a person do if he/she is asked to pay for a hypothetical CV scenario given their budget or income constraint?

While conducting surveys may look easy, to some it is not. Doing surveys is an art that requires good people and communication skills as well as a keenness for details. Hence, enumerators must have adequate interview skills to obtain accurate and relevant information from the respondents.

Whittington (2002) suggested some tips for good interview practice, particularly on how enumerators ought to ask different types of questions, based on his experience in conducting CV surveys in developing countries (Table A6.1).

Also, enumerators need to make relevant observations by taking notes of important information shared by the respondent that is related to the survey but not asked in the questionnaire.

Table A6.1: Rules for a Good Interview Practice

No.	Advice	Comment
1	Read every question exactly as written in the questionnaire. Do not improvise.	Research on the art of asking questions shows that precise wording of questions may significantly affect the respondents' answers. If each enumerator develops their way of asking questions, one can never be sure that the same question is asked. We need to make sure that each respondent is answering the same question. Reading the question exactly also makes the interview shorter.
2	Read the question slowly enough so that the respondent can understand.	An enumerator has seen the questions a hundred times before. It is natural for the enumerator to want to go quickly over a question that they know so well, but which the respondent hears for the first time. Thus, the enumerator needs to speak slowly.
3	Wait for the respondent to answer.	Some enumerators will read the question once, then look up and repeat the question, and sometimes even start a lengthy explanation, before letting the respondent answer. Ask once very clearly and let the respondent think.
4	If the respondent can't answer, repeat the question.	The respondent may not have been paying attention the first time. If after repeating the question, the respondent does not still get it, move to the next question.
5	Remain neutral about the respondents' answers. Do not influence their answer.	Never express surprise, disapproval, judgment, or doubt about a response. Do not let your facial expression change. Just record the answer. For example, if the respondent says they would be willing to pay a very large amount for a good or service, the enumerator should not say, "WOW!". If the respondent gives a factually wrong answer, the enumerator should not reveal that they know the answer is incorrect.
6	Do not act embarrassed at the respondents' answer to sensitive questions.	This will increase the embarrassment of the respondent, not reduce it. Be very matter of fact.

continued on next page

Table A6.1 (continued)

No.	Advice	Comment
7	Never suggest an answer unless the instruction says you must read the answers to the respondents.	For example, if the respondent is having difficulty estimating their income, do not prompt with a question like, "Is your income more than ___/month? Is it ____?"
8	Do not repeat the respondents' answer.	This is a waste of time unless you may want to clarify if you got their response right.
9	Do not advise respondents on personal matters.	Enumerators should refer respondents to the appropriate authorities for questions that may arise that are not within the scope of the interview.
10	Directly answer the question that the respondent may have about the purpose of the survey.	Respondents are entitled to know the purpose of the survey and how they have been selected for the interview. The enumerator should not be reluctant to take time to provide a clear, detailed answer to such questions.
11	Listen carefully to the respondents' answer.	It is very off-putting to the respondent if the enumerator is not very attentive. Moreover, the respondent may be offering an answer, which may be different from what it appears to be. In such cases, the enumerator must listen carefully to the respondent.

Source: ADB (2013).

Appendix 7: Regression Models Commonly Used for Analyzing CVM Data

This appendix discusses common regression models for analyzing CVM data. These models make up the technical framework behind the practical implementation discussed in the main text. These include frameworks for the single-bounded dichotomous choice model (SBDC), the double-bounded dichotomous choice model (DBCM), payment card, and the multiple-bound discrete choice model (MBDC).

Single-Bounded Dichotomous Choice Model

The basic empirical model for discrete choice models is the random utility model. The model starts with a status quo indirect utility, V_0, which has two components: a deterministic component and a random (or error) component. Assuming a linear specification for the status quo, indirect utility, V_0, for an individual can be written as:

$$V_0 = \gamma_0 + \sum_K \gamma_{0k} X_k + \gamma_{0Y} Y + \varepsilon_0$$

In this equation, X_k are variables that are thought to affect the utility of the individual, and Y is the income level of the individual. These components along with the intercept, γ_0, are the deterministic part of the indirect utility. The term, ε, on the other hand, is the error term that accounts for other factors that may have been excluded from the specification and, in general, reflects the analyst's uncertainty of the respondent's preferences. That is, these are components of the individual or respondent's utility that is known to him/her but not to the analyst. This last term is the stochastic or random component of the indirect utility function.

The post-CV scenario indirect utility function, V1, on the other hand, can be written as:

$$V1 = \gamma 1 + \sum_K \gamma_{1k} X_k + \gamma_{1Y} (Y - b) + \varepsilon_1$$

The components and variables of this indirect utility are the same as described in the status quo indirect utility function except for two things. First, the bid price b is introduced; and second, the error term is different.

A respondent will agree or say yes to an offered bid (or vote yes in a voting referendum) if the utility from the program or policy is greater than the utility from the status quo, i.e.,

$$V_1 = \gamma_1 + \sum_K \gamma 1k\, X_k + \gamma_{1Y}(Y - b) + \varepsilon_1 > V_0 = \gamma_0 + \sum_K \gamma_{0k} X_k + \gamma_{0Y} Y + \varepsilon_0$$

Simplifying this relationship would lead to the following expression of the change in utility (ΔV):

$$\Delta V = V_1 - V_0 = \beta_0 + \sum_K \beta_k X_k - \gamma_{1Y} b + \varepsilon > 0$$

Here, $\beta_0 = \gamma_1$; $\beta_k = \gamma_{1k}$, and $\varepsilon_1 - \varepsilon_0$. Notice that the income of the respondent drops out of the relationship. This is because the marginal utility of income for an individual is more likely to be constant across the status quo and the policy/program change scenario especially when the bid or cost is small relative to the income, i.e., $\gamma_{1Y} = \gamma_{0Y}$. This is a drawback of the linear specification for the indirect utility function. However, the linear specification is a good approximation to any arbitrary utility specification and has been the workhorse in CV literature (Haab and McConnell 2002).

Since income is an important determinant of demand and choice, it would be hard not to include it in any discrete choice specification. One way to address this specification problem in a theoretically consistent way is to specify a varying parameters model. The simplest way to apply this specification is to use categories for income, which could be income ranges used in national poverty studies or a modified version that is suitable for the study area. As Haab and McConnell (2002) argued, it is more plausible for the marginal utility of income to vary across individuals rather than across states for an individual. In essence, each group will have its marginal utility of income. Thus, the utility change (ΔV) can be rewritten as

$$\Delta V = V_1 - V_0 = \beta_0 + \sum_K \beta_k X_k + \sum_I \beta_{Yi} Y_i - \gamma_{1Y} b + \varepsilon > 0$$

Where Y_i represents an income category i (or a specific income range). As usual, one category is dropped in the specification to avoid multicollinearity.

The probability of agreeing to a bid or vote yes in a referendum can therefore be written as:

$$Pr(yes) = Pr\left(\left(\beta_0 + \sum_K \beta_k X_k + \sum_I \beta_{Yi} Y_i - \gamma_{1Y} b + \varepsilon\right) > 0\right)$$

$$Pr(yes) = Pr\left(-\left(\beta_0 + \sum_K \beta_k X_k + \sum_I \beta_{Yi} Y_i - \gamma_{1Y} b\right) < \varepsilon\right)$$

The commonly used distributions are the logistic and normal distributions. These distributional assumptions along with the assumption that the error term, ε, is independent and identically distributed complete most of the specification in the literature. Because both the logistic and normal distributions are symmetric, we can rewrite the previous equation as:

$$Pr(yes) = Pr\left(\left(\beta_0 + \sum_K \beta_k X_k + \sum_I \beta_{Yi} Y_i - \gamma_{1Y} b\right) > \varepsilon\right)$$

If $\varepsilon \sim N(0,\sigma^2)$ or is assumed to follow a normal distribution, then the probability of saying yes to an offered bid can be expressed as:

$$Pr(yes) = Pr\left(\left(\beta_0 + \sum_K \beta_k X_k + \sum_I \beta_{Yi} Y_i - \gamma_{1Y} b\right) > \varepsilon\right)$$

$$= Pr\left(\left(\frac{\beta_0}{\sigma} + \sum_K \frac{\beta_k}{\sigma} X_k + \sum_I \frac{\beta_{Yi}}{\sigma} Y_i - \frac{\gamma_{1Y}}{\sigma} b\right) > \frac{\varepsilon}{\sigma}\right)$$

$$= \Phi\left(\left(\frac{\beta_0}{\sigma} + \sum_K \frac{\beta_k}{\sigma} X_k + \sum_I \frac{\beta_{Yi}}{\sigma} Y_i - \frac{\gamma_{1Y}}{\sigma} b\right) > \frac{\varepsilon}{\sigma}\right)$$

The last equation follows from the usual conversion of $\varepsilon \sim N(0,\sigma^2)$ to a standard normal distribution, i.e., $\varepsilon \sim N(0,1)$. The standard normal distribution is represented by the $\Phi(\cdot)$ function. On the other hand, if the error term is assumed to follow a logistic distribution, the probability of agreeing to a bid is given by:

$$Pr(yes) = \frac{1}{1+e^{-\left(\frac{\beta_0}{\sigma} + \sum_K \frac{\beta_k}{\sigma} X_k + \sum_I \frac{\beta_{Yi}}{\sigma} Y_i - \frac{\gamma_{1Y}}{\sigma} b\right)}}$$

Measuring the Willingness to Pay for the Single-Bounded Dichotomous Choice Model

Deriving the estimate for the willingness to pay for the good or benefit produced by a project or policy is the end point of estimating the parameters of the change in the indirect utility function. The estimation of the WTP is connected to the estimated parameters from either a probit or logit regression. As defined earlier, a respondent's value or WTP for goods or benefits produced by a project or policy can be written as:

$$\Delta V = V_1 - V_0 = \beta_0 + \sum \beta_k X_k + \sum \beta_{Yi} Y_i - \gamma_{1Y} WTP + \varepsilon = 0$$

Here the variables are the same as those defined in the previous sections, except for replacing the bid variable with the WTP variable. To calculate for the WTP, we use the following equation:

$$WTP = \frac{(\beta_0 + \Sigma_K \beta_k X_k + \Sigma_I \beta_{Yi} Y_i)}{\gamma_{1Y}} + \frac{\varepsilon}{\gamma_{1Y}}$$

To obtain the central tendencies of the WTP estimate, the mean and median WTP are the measures most commonly used. Since ε is either distributed as a standard normal or as a logistic distribution, the mean and the median are equal. Furthermore, ε is assumed to have a mean of zero. Thus, when the expected value of WTP is taken, we have:

$$E[WTP|\beta_0, \beta_k, \gamma \backslash 1Y] = \frac{\beta_0 + \Sigma_K \beta_k X_k + \Sigma_I \beta_{Yi} Y_i}{\gamma_{1Y}}$$

Consistent estimates of the parameters from the probit or logit regressions are used in estimating the WTP. Using this information, the expected WTP can be expressed as:

$$E[WTP|\beta_0, \beta_k, \gamma_{1Y}] = \frac{\widehat{\beta_0} + \Sigma_K \widehat{\beta_k} X_k + \Sigma_I \widehat{\beta_{Yi}} Y_i}{\widehat{\gamma_{1Y}}}$$

$\widehat{\beta_0}$, $\widehat{\beta_k}$, $\widehat{\beta_{Yi}}$ and $\widehat{\gamma_{1Y}}$ are the estimated parameters from the regressions. There are two options for computing E[WTP]: the first is to compute the individual WTP and take its mean, and the second is to use the mean of the socioeconomic and behavioral variables.

Computing the Mean Willingness to Pay from an SBDC Model

Based on the derivations above, the mean or expected willingness to pay can be calculated using the estimated parameters from the regressions. Table A7.1 shows how this formula works after a probit regression.

Table A7.1: Computing the Mean Willingness to Pay from SBDC

Variable	Coefficient (β_i)	Mean (X^o)	Coefficient*Mean ($\beta_i X$)
Income	0.00002	24,501.0	0.48468
Education	-0.00826	10.60700	-0.08765
Gender	0.04213	0.49380	0.02080
Age	-0.01020	43.27100	-0.44149
Dwelling	0.11087	0.58058	0.06437
Yard	0.00146	121.68000	0.17805
Impact	-0.07108	4.38220	-0.31146
Quality	-0.12587	3.04340	-0.38307
Regression constant	1.89640	1	1.89640
		Total	1.42062
Bid price	-0.19779	...	
Mean WTP		1.42062/-019779*-1	7.18246

Source: Gunatilake et al. (2007).

Therefore, the mean WTP can be calculated by simply multiplying the estimated coefficients by their respective variables and dividing it by the absolute value of the bid coefficient. It is important to note that the numerator contains the sum of the products of all the estimated coefficients and the corresponding variable except that of the bid. We can also calculate the WTP for each respondent and take the mean WTP for the whole sample. As an alternative, the mean values of the regressors can be used, and multiplied by the associated estimated parameters.

Obtaining the expected value of the WTP addresses the variations caused by preference uncertainty which is a result of the random utility specification of the indirect utility function. There are two other potential sources of variation in the WTP: those brought about by individual characteristics of respondents or observed heterogeneity and those resulting from the uncertainty because of the randomness of the parameters. Randomness in parameters occurs when maximum likelihood is used to estimate the parameters of the standard normal or logistic distributions.

Observed heterogeneity can easily be addressed by including behavioral and socioeconomic characteristics in the specification of indirect utility. The randomness of parameters, on the other hand, can be dealt with by computing the standard deviation which is a nonlinear function of different values of the parameters. There are several ways to address the randomness of parameters and construct a confidence interval (CI) for the WTP estimate: (i) the delta method, (ii) the Krinsky-Robb (KR) approach, and (iii) the use of bootstrapping. The delta method uses a first-order Taylor series approximation of the E[WTP] equation derived above. But the delta method[2] may be inappropriate since it only produces symmetric CIs (Jeanty 2007). The KR[3] and bootstrapping are similar in calculating the WTP using the E[WTP] equation, as both draw samples either from the parameter distribution or from the observations. KR draws from the asymptotic normal distribution of the parameter estimates, while the bootstrap method resamples from the observations and estimates new parameter values from each resampling. It is also recommended to show the confidence interval of the WTP estimates from either of these two methods.

Double-Bounded Dichotomous Choice Model

The manner by which the $\widehat{WTP}$ is elicited in the double-bounded dichotomous choice model leads to the following four possible responses:

a) Respondent agrees with the first offered bid (b_1) but does not agree with the second bid (b_2) [Y-N]. What is known with this response pattern is first that $b_2 > b_1$. Second, if WTP^* is the true WTP of the respondent, then it is bounded by the two bids, i.e., $b_1 \leq WTP^* < b_2$.

b) Respondent does not agree with the first offered bid (b_1) but agrees with the second bid (b_2) [N-Y]. What is known with this response pattern is first that $b_1 > b_2$. Then WTP^* is bounded by the two bids, i.e., $b_2 \leq WTP^* < b_1$.

c) Respondent agrees with both bids b_1 and b_2 [Y-Y]. Then the true WTP is not bounded from above, i.e., $b_2 \leq WTP^* < \infty$.

d) Respondent does not agree with both bids b_1 and b_2 [N-N]. Then the true WTP is bounded by 0 and b_1, i.e., $0 < WTP^* < b_1$.

2 This can be implemented using the nlcom command in Stata®.

3 The Krinsky-Robb approach to constructing a WTP confidence interval can be implemented in Stata® through the user-written command wtpcikr and wtp.

Since more information and data points are provided by the DBDC elicitation format, it is thus considered to be more efficient. Notice also that when there are response changes, i.e., Y-N and N-Y responses, the true WTP is bounded by the offered bids. Even when there are consistent response patterns, i.e., Y-Y and N-N, there is an added restriction in the possible distribution of the true WTP.

Suppose the true WTP of a respondent is given by:

$$WTP^* = \alpha_0 + \sum_K \alpha_k X_k + \sum_I \alpha_{Yi} Y_i + \varepsilon$$

The variables are defined similarly to the SBDC format discussed in the text, but we have changed the notations for the parameters to be estimated. Notice also the explicit assumption that the WTP and the error term are the same for both the first and second bid offer or both CV questions.

If the assumption that $\varepsilon \sim N(0,\sigma^2)$ is maintained, the probabilities of observing the four patterns can be represented by the following joint probabilities:

$$Prob(Yes,No) = Prob(b_1 \leq WTP^* < b_2)$$

$$Prob(Yes,No) = Prob\left(b_1 \leq \left(\alpha_0 + \sum_K \alpha_k X_k + \sum_I \alpha_{Yi} Y_i + \varepsilon\right) < b_2\right)$$

$$= Prob\left(\frac{b_1 - [\alpha_0 + \Sigma_K \alpha_k X_k + \Sigma_I \alpha_{Yi} Y_i]}{\sigma}\right) \leq + \frac{\varepsilon}{\sigma}$$

$$< \left(\frac{b_2 - [\alpha_0 + \Sigma_K \alpha_k X_k + \Sigma_I \alpha_{Yi} Y_i]}{\sigma}\right)$$

$$= \Phi\left(\frac{\alpha_0 + \Sigma_K \alpha_k X_k + \Sigma_I \alpha_{Yi} Y_i - b_1}{\sigma}\right)$$

$$-\Phi\left(\frac{\alpha_0 + \Sigma_K \alpha_k X_k + \Sigma_I \alpha_{Yi} Y_i - b_2}{\sigma}\right)$$

The last equality is obtained from the symmetric properties of the normal distribution, $\Phi(\cdot)$. Similarly, the probability of observing an N-Y pattern is expressed as:

$$Prob(No, Yes) = \Phi\left(\frac{\alpha_0 + \Sigma_K \alpha_k X_k + \Sigma_I \alpha_{Yi} Y_i - b_2}{\sigma}\right)$$

$$-\Phi\left(\frac{\alpha_0 + \Sigma_K \alpha_k X_k + \Sigma_I \alpha_{Yi} Y_i - b_1}{\sigma}\right)$$

On the other hand, the probability of having a Y-Y response pattern is given by:

$$Prob(Yes,Yes) = Prob\left(b_1 \leq \left(\alpha_0 + \sum_K \alpha_k X_k + \sum_I \alpha_{Yi} Y_i + \varepsilon,\ b_2\right) \leq \left(\alpha_0 + \sum_K \alpha_k X_k + \sum_I \alpha_{Yi} Y_i + \varepsilon\right)\right)$$

Applying the Bayes rule and recognizing the symmetry of the normal distribution, we can rewrite the previous equation as:

$$Prob(Yes, Yes) = \Phi\left(\frac{\alpha_0 + \sum_K \alpha_k X_k + \sum_I \alpha_{Yi} Y_i - b_2}{\sigma}\right)$$

Employing the same derivation, the probability of an N-N response pattern is given by:

$$Prob(No, No) = 1 - \Phi\left(\frac{\alpha_0 + \sum_K \alpha_k X_k + \sum_I \alpha_{Yi} Y_i - b_2}{\sigma}\right)$$

Estimating the parameters for the DBDC is not as straightforward as in the SBDC format. It would require setting up a log-likelihood function, which is defined by the four equations derived earlier. The parameters of the model (α_0, α_k, α_{Yi}) are then estimated by maximizing the log-likelihood function for these parameters.[4] As an alternative, the interval regression model can be used for the econometric specification for the DBDC elicitation format.

Once the parameters are estimated, the WTP can be computed using the same procedure for the payment card format discussed in the next section. Thus,

$$mean\ WTP = \exp\left(\beta' X + \frac{\sigma^2}{2}\right)$$

Note that unlike in the probit estimation of the SDBC, the standard error of the disturbance or error term, ε, is directly estimated.

An alternative econometric model for the DBDC format allows for different WTPs for the first and second questions.

[4] Double b is a user-written program in Stata® that estimates the parameters of a DBDC format using this approach.

$$WTP_1 = \alpha_{01} + \sum_K \alpha_{k1} X_k + \sum_I \alpha_{Yi1} Y_i + \varepsilon_1$$

$$WTP_2 = \alpha_{02} + \sum \alpha_{k2} X_k + \sum \alpha_{Yi2} Y_i + \varepsilon_2$$

Here, WTP_1 is the WTP-generating process for the first bid offer, and WTP_2 is for the second bid offer. While the variables are the same for the first and second WTP equations, the parameters may or may not be the same. The error terms are assumed to be distributed normally, i.e., $\varepsilon_1 \sim N(0,\sigma_1^2)$ and $\varepsilon_1 \sim N(0,\sigma_2^2)$. The error terms are also allowed to be correlated through a covariance parameter σ_{12}. With these distributional assumptions, maximum likelihood estimation of a bivariate probit can be used for this econometric model .

The process of estimating the WTP measure is the same as that of the SDBC format described earlier. However, this econometric model can yield two different WTP estimates. The researcher is now faced with the choice of deciding which WTP measure is more appropriate, without any clear statistical guideline. Another complication is that if the estimated covariance is $\sigma_{12}=0$, there is no correlation between the two error terms. This would lead to independent probit models which can then be estimated separately. Thus, the efficiency gains from the DBDC format are lost.

A possible solution to both problems is to implement a two-stage estimation. In the first stage, a bivariate probit is estimated, and a test is done on the equality of the parameters across both equations. If the parameters are not significantly different across equations, this can be used as a cross-equation constraint. The second stage would be to estimate a constrained bivariate probit. In this way, the efficiency gains of the DBDC format are still maintained and at the same time, only one WTP needs to be calculated. But this depends heavily on being able to impose the cross-equation constraints.

Payment Card

The payment card elicitation format, as described in the main text, lets the respondent choose from a list or set of bids. Suppose that a respondent is offered a list of ascending bids (b_{min}, b_p, ..., b_{max}). These bids serve as an ordered set of critical or threshold values that bound the respondent's true willingness to pay. If the respondent picks bid b_k, then his true WTP is in between this bid (b_k) and the next higher bid (b_{k+1}). Thus, the probability that the respondent picks this bid is equivalent to the probability that his true WTP lies in between bid b_k and the next higher bid, b_{k+1}. Thus,

$$Prob(choose\ b_k) = Prob(b_k \leq WTP < b_{k+1})$$

The true WTP is an unobserved latent variable that is assumed to be linearly determined by a vector of covariates X, and a random component $\varepsilon_1 \sim N(0,\sigma^2)$, i.e.,

$$WTP = \beta' X + \varepsilon$$

Then we can rewrite the probability of choosing b_k as:

$$Prob(choose\ b_k) = \Phi\left(\frac{b_{K+1} - \beta' X}{\sigma^2}\right) - \Phi\left(\frac{b_K - \beta' X}{\sigma^2}\right)$$

Here, Φ is the standard normal CDF.

Interval Midpoint and Minimum Lower Bound

Since the respondent's true WTP is assumed to be systematically distributed between the chosen bid and the next higher bid, the dependent variable can be a point estimate. The dependent variable can either assume the value of the chosen bid or alternatively the midpoint of the interval. This assumption leads to a continuous dependent variable. At the outset, ordinary least squares (OLS) can be used to estimate the parameters. However, it is highly likely that these constructed dependent variables are censored. Censoring occurs because the minimum lower bound or interval midpoint values are constrained within a range, i.e., $b_k \varepsilon [b_{min}, b_{max}]$. Thus, the latent or unobserved true WTP is assumed to have the following value:

$$WTP = \begin{cases} b_k \text{ if } b_{min} <_k < b_{max} \\ b_{min} \text{ if } WTP \leq b_{min} \\ b_{max} \text{ if } WTP \geq b_{max} \end{cases}$$

For the example discussed in the text (see section 6.3), using the minimum lower bound as the WTP point estimate would mean b_{min} = 0, while for the interval midpoint b_{min} = 25.

The Tobit regression model is appropriate under these conditions, as it utilizes a maximum likelihood estimation of a log-likelihood equation, which accounts for left and right censoring of the dependent variable. If we indicate respondents whose WTP $\leq b_{min}$ (i.e., left censored observations) as observations $i \varepsilon L$, observations or respondents whose WTP $\leq b_{max}$ (i.e., right censored observations) as observations $i \varepsilon R$, and respondents with $b_{min} < b_k < b_{max}$ as $i \varepsilon UC$, then the log-likelihood of observing the data could be written as:

$$\ln L = \sum_{i \varepsilon L} \log\Phi\left(\frac{b_{min,i} - \beta' X}{\sigma}\right) + 1/2 \sum_{i \varepsilon UC} \log \left\{\left(\frac{b_{K,i} - \beta' X}{\sigma}\right)^2 + \log 2\pi\sigma^2\right\}$$

$$+ \sum_{i \varepsilon R} \log \left(1 - \Phi\left(\frac{b_{max,i} - \beta' X}{\sigma}\right)\right)$$

Maximizing this log-likelihood with respect to the elements of the vector of coefficients β, and σ results in estimates of the WTP function.

Interval Data

The constructed intervals that bound the payment or bid choice can also be used as the dependent variable. Interval data are left and right censored, for the first and last interval, respectively. Given this, suppose we have respondents $i\varepsilon L$ who are left censored, $i\varepsilon R$ who are right-censored observations, and respondents $i\varepsilon T$ who are intervals. Cameron and Huppert (1989) suggest the following log-normal specification to avoid negative WTP:

$$\log WTP = \beta' X + \varepsilon$$

Then the log-likelihood is:

$$\ln L = \sum_{i \varepsilon L} \log\Phi\left(\frac{b_{min,i} - \beta' X}{\sigma}\right) + \sum_{i \varepsilon T} \log\left\{\Phi\left(\frac{\log b_{K+1,i} - \beta' X}{\sigma}\right) 1 - \Phi\left(\frac{b_{max,i} - \beta' X}{\sigma}\right)\right\}$$

$$+ \sum_{i \varepsilon U} \log \left(1 - \Phi\left(\frac{\log b_{max,i} - \beta' X}{\sigma}\right)\right.$$

Again, maximizing this log-likelihood function with respect to the elements of the vector of coefficients β, and ,σ results in the estimates of the WTP function.

For interval data the appropriate regression model is the interval regression. To implement this in Stata, variables containing the upper and lower bound of each interval will need to be generated first. For the first interval, the lower bound should be assigned a missing value, and the upper bound of the last interval should also be assigned a missing value. The interval regression is facilitated by the *intreg* command in Stata.

Given the log-normal specification for the WTP function, the mean WTP can be derived using the following formula:

$$\text{mean WTP} = \exp\left(\widehat{\beta'}X + \frac{\widehat{\sigma^2}}{2}\right)$$

Where $\widehat{\beta}$ and $\widehat{\sigma^2}$ are the coefficients and the variance that is estimated from the interval regression.

Ordered Categories

The dependent variable can also be treated as ordered categories. Suppose that the payments (or ascending intervals) are labeled as ordered categories j=1, 2, J, then the probability that respondent *I* chooses category j can be represented by:

$$\begin{aligned} Pr(y_i = j) &= Pr(k_{j-1} < \beta' X + \varepsilon < k_j) \\ &= \Phi(k_j - \beta' X) - \Phi(k_{j-1} - \beta' X) \end{aligned}$$

The log-likelihood of observing the data for respondents i=1, N is given by:

$$\ln L = \sum_{j=1}^{J} \sum_{i=1}^{N} I_j(y_i) \log\left\{\Phi\left(\frac{k_j - \beta' X}{\sigma}\right) - \Phi\left(\frac{k_{j-1} - \beta' X}{\sigma}\right)\right\}$$

Where $I_j(y_i)$ is an indicator variable that has the following value:

$$I_j(y_i) = \begin{cases} 1, & \text{if } y_i = j \\ 0, & \text{otherwise} \end{cases}$$

The ordered probit regression is the appropriate model when the dependent variable is an ordered categorical variable. This can be implemented in Stata using the *oprobit* command. To prepare the data set for the ordered regression in Stata, the dependent variable should be converted to categories that represent the different intervals.

Multiple-Bound Dichotomous Choice Model

The multiple-bound discrete choice (MBDC) elicitation format as described in Chapter 6, incorporates uncertainty explicitly into the payment card bid format. Unlike the payment card format, the respondent is shown the whole bid or payment range and is asked to express his/her uncertainty qualitatively over each bid/payment. For example, if there are three bid values, 0, 50, and 100, for each bid, the respondent is asked whether he/she is not paying, probably not paying, not sure of paying, probably paying, or definitely paying. Thus, the respondent's uncertainty is expressed through these categorical degrees.[5]

There are several regression models that have been used to analyze contingent valuation data from an MBDC elicitation format. Welsh and Poe (1998) used a recoding of the CV data to form an interval that bounds the respondent's true WTP. In particular, the "probably paying" and "definitely paying" are considered as yes "votes," while other categorical degrees are treated as no "votes." The lower bound of the interval is the highest bid/payment for which the respondent gave a "probably paying" or "definitely paying" response. The upper bound of the interval is the next higher bid or payment in which a no "vote" is indicated. This interval becomes the dependent variable in an interval regression. The implementation in Stata and the derivation of the mean WTP are the same as the interval data regression for the payment card elicitation format. It is worth noting that since the WTP is being bounded by two bid values, the MBDC also shares some similarity with the DBDC discussed earlier. The main difference is that the bid or payments are all visible to the respondent under the MBDC, while in the DBDC the subsequent bid is revealed only after the first CV question.

Alberini et al. (2003, p. 41) criticized Welsh and Poe (1998) in that they "assume that responses to the multiple bids were driven by a unique willingness to pay (WTP) for each respondent and that all information about WTP is revealed by the bid intervals where responses switch from 'yes' to 'no'." Alberini et al. (2003) used a panel data probit to allow unrestricted correlation across the respondent's responses. They used the same recoding procedure of Welsh and Poe (1988), but instead of identifying an interval, they retained all bid or payment responses for each respondent. Thus, they created a panel data of binary or yes/no responses, which allowed for correlation of a respondent's responses across the bids or payments.

[5] Alternatively, the uncertainty can be expressed quantitatively by assigning numerical probabilities to the qualitative categories. This version is called the stochastic payment card elicitation format. Interested readers can look at the work of Wang and Whittington (2005) for further details.

A random effects probit regression model was used to estimate the parameters of the WTP function. The mean WTP is calculated like that of the SBDC elicitation format.

Alberini et al. (2003) also proposed and used the ordered probit regression model in analyzing MBDC data. They treated each bid response as a polychotomous choice and called it the random valuation model. The advantage of this is that uncertainty response categories are explicitly accounted for in the analysis. Welsh and Poe (1998) and the random effects probit model of Alberini et al. (2003) essentially assume away uncertainty by recoding to certain responses. The drawback of this is that the correlation between responses is not accounted for, unlike in the random effects probit model.

Photo Credits

Page 1 (Left to right, top to bottom): Sita Maya Syangbo drinking water is supplied by the Bharatpur drinking water board in Nepal (photo by Samir Jung Thapa); Cil Yu Ha Vuong, 72, patrols the forests with fellow community members of the ADB-funded Poverty and Environment Fund – The Biodiversity Corridor Program (photo by Lester Ledesma); A villager from Da Nhim, Viet Nam rounds up cattle from nearby grazing grounds (photo by Lester Ledesma); Mangrove management training in the Philippines (photo by Eric Sales); A school of colorful fishes brightens marine life in Batangas, Philippines (photo by Brian Manuel).

Page 7 (Left to right, top to bottom): A project team holds a focus group discussion for a CVM study in Bataan, Philippines (photo by Dan Diona); A team meets to discuss the South Tarawa Sanitation Improvement Sector Project in Kiribati (photo by Eric Sales).

Page 41 (Left to right, top to bottom): Studying location maps around Macooih forests, Viet Nam (photo by Lester Ledesma); Preparatory and qualitative pretesting of a CV questionnaire in Bataan, Philippines (photo by Arielle Fajardo).

Page 52: Samples of CVM questionnaires (photo by Jindra Nuella Samson).

Page 73 (Left to right, top to bottom): A farmer recalls survey field work in Nueva Ecija, Philippines (photo by R-CDTA 8369 Project Team); Residents of Baros and Krakahan, Indonesia conduct a cognitive mapping exercise (photo by Cheryl Fernandez); Pretesting a CV questionnaire in Bataan, Philippines (photo by Asa Jose Sajise).

Page 89 (Left to right, top to bottom): Sub editor with face mask and gloves works at his office in Dhaka, Bangladesh (photo by Abir Abdullah); Focus group discussion at Bataan National Park in Bataan, Philippines (photo by Dan Z. Diona); Logit regression output in Stata (photo by Asa Jose Sajise).

Page 122 (Left to right, top to bottom): ADB team members meet with members of the Woman's Self Help Group in South Adampur Village, West Bengal, India; An engineer surveys the new asphalt installation at an embankment of a road improvement project in Bangladesh (photo by Gerhard Joren); GIS technology is used to collect field data in Nueva Ecija, Philippines (photo by R-CDTA 8369 project team).

www.ingramcontent.com/pod-product-compliance
Lightning Source LLC
Chambersburg PA
CBHW040256290326
41929CB00052B/3432

* 9 7 8 9 2 9 2 6 9 2 7 5 9 *